the series on school reform

| Patricia A. Wasley | Ann Lieberman | Joseph P. McDonald |
| University of Washington | NCREST | New York University |

SERIES EDITORS

The Power of Protocols:
An Educator's Guide to Better Practice
    JOSEPH P. McDONALD,
    NANCY MOHR, ALAN DICHTER, AND
    ELIZABETH C. McDONALD

Beating the Odds:
High Schools as Communities of Commitment
    JACQUELINE ANCESS

At the Heart of Teaching:
A Guide to Reflective Practice
    GRACE HALL McENTEE, JON APPLEBY,
    JOANNE DOWD, JAN GRANT, SIMON HOLE,
    AND PEGGY SILVA, WITH JOSEPH W. CHECK

Teaching Youth Media: A Critical Guide to
Literacy, Video Production, & Social Change
    STEVEN GOODMAN

Inside the National Writing Project: Connecting
Network Learning and Classrooms
    ANN LIEBERMAN AND
    DIANE WOOD

Standards Reform in High-Poverty Schools:
Managing Conflict and Building Capacity
    CAROL A. BARNES

Standards of Mind and Heart:
Creating the Good High School
    PEGGY SILVA AND ROBERT A. MACKIN

Upstart Startup: Creating and
Sustaining a Public Charter School
    JAMES NEHRING

One Kid at a Time:
Big Lessons from a Small School
    ELIOT LEVINE

Guiding School Change:
The Role and Work of Change Agents
    FRANCES O'CONNELL RUST AND
    HELEN FREIDUS, EDITORS

Teachers Caught in the Action:
Professional Development That Matters
    ANN LIEBERMAN AND
    LYNNE MILLER, EDITORS

The Competent Classroom:
Aligning High School Curriculum, Standards, and
Assessment—A Creative Teaching Guide
    ALLISON ZMUDA AND
    MARY TOMAINO

Central Park East and Its Graduates:
"Learning by Heart"
    DAVID BENSMAN

Taking Charge of Curriculum: Teacher Networks
and Curriculum Implementation
    JACOB E. ADAMS, JR.

Teaching With Power:
Shared Decision-Making and Classroom Practice
    CAROL REED

Good Schools/Real Schools:
Why School Reform Doesn't Last
    DEAN FINK

Beyond Formulas in Mathematics and Teaching:
Dynamics of the High School Algebra Classroom
    DANIEL CHAZAN

School Reform Behind the Scenes
    JOSEPH P. McDONALD, THOMAS HATCH,
    EDWARD KIRBY, NANCY AMES, NORRIS M.
    HAYNES, AND EDWARD T. JOYNER

Looking Together at Student Work:
A Companion Guide to Assessing Student Learning
    TINA BLYTHE, DAVID ALLEN, AND
    BARBARA SHIEFFELIN POWELL

Looking at Student Work:
A Window into the Classroom (Video)
    ANNENBERG INSTITUTE FOR SCHOOL
    REFORM

Teachers—Transforming Their World and Their Work
    ANN LIEBERMAN AND
    LYNNE MILLER

Teaching in Common: Challenges to Joint Work
in Classrooms and Schools
    ANNE DiPARDO

Charter Schools: Another Flawed Educational Reform?
    SEYMOUR B. SARASON

(Continued)

the series on school reform, *continued*

The Power of Protocols

An Educator's Guide to Better Practice

Joseph P. McDonald
Nancy Mohr
Alan Dichter
Elizabeth C. McDonald

Teachers College
Columbia University
New York and London

For Hannah and Bert
faithful witnesses
to our writing weekends in Wareham

Published by Teachers College Press, 1234 Amsterdam Avenue, New York, NY 10027.

Copyright © 2003 by Teachers College, Columbia University

Library of Congress Cataloging-in-Publication Data

The power of protocols : an educator's guide to better practice / Joseph P. McDonald...
[et al.].
    p. cm. — (The series on school reform)
    Includes bibliographical references and index.
    ISBN 0-8077-4362-3 (cloth) — ISBN 0-8077-4361-5 (pbk.)
        1. High schools—United States—Examinations. 2. Educational tests and
    measurements—United States. 3. Grading and marking (Students) —
United States. 4. Teachers—United States—Training of. I. McDonald, Joseph P.
II. Series.

    LB3060.285.U6.P69 2003
    373.1102—dc21   2002072103

    ISBN 0-8077-4361-5 (paper)
    ISBN 0-8077-4362-3 (cloth)
    Printed on acid-free paper
    Manufactured in the United States of America
    10 09 08 07 06 05   8 7 6 5 4

Contents

FOREWORD

Why Use Protocols?

Planning as a "Real" Team

To say that I was skeptical would be understating my initial reaction to the notion of applying formulated protocols to the tasks of collaborative planning. An earlier, unhappy experience with School-based Management/Shared Decision-Making had deteriorated into an ugly power struggle between the teachers' union on one side and the school administration and parents' organization on the other–despite the application of Robert's Rules of Order. Given the charge to make the State-mandated School Leadership Team work successfully, however, I was persuaded by colleagues, successful principals, and professional trainers of a much less traditional stripe than I, to give the protocols at least a chance. And what a revelation it proved to be! After undertaking to learn and introduce them to our team, I was astonished to see them at work. Such formats as a Go-round and the Tuning Protocol gave even the most reticent of our team members a voice, and limited the dominance of the more assertive who had intimidated them. Disagreements became challenges to be resolved rather than arguments, thanks to the protocols of "warm" and "cool" (never "cruel") responses, enabling discussion while maintaining focus on shared vision and goals. Moreover, the team actually began to function as a "team," with each member relaxing into the dual roles of active listener and contributor as they became more comfortable with the protocol models of group process.

Harris Sarney
Principal, Bayside High School, Queens, New York City

Bridging Cultures

In preparing for Principal-for-a-Day I was paired with Jane Pauley of NBC and told to work on creating a partnership with her organization—one which clearly had a completely different culture from that of a high school in New York City. As my palms sweated, I waited for Jane's keen questioning tactics. But it was through the use of a protocol that the bridging of our two cultures could begin. We were led through a Descriptive Consultancy Protocol, in which we each talked about our hopes and our fears about working together. We did this at a "fishbowl" where other Principal-for-a-Day folks watched. I remember Jane saying that she particularly valued the "focused listening" that was involved. The protocol directed our concentration, our speaking and, most importantly, provided a focus for our listening across our organizations.

Ada Rosario-Dolch
Principal, High School for Leadership and Public Service
New York City

Confronting Issues of Diversity

I am an African American woman and educator with many years experience teaching English in urban high schools, and also working with other educators in urban areas. More often than not I use articles by Gloria Ladson-Billings or Lisa Delpit and do text-based discussions such as the Final Word. Some mainstream, White educators are not used to seeing the words *White* and *Black* referenced in an article and are angry that we are even having a conversation about race, class, and gender. On the other hand, if the group is a diverse group, then the article must be passionate, relevant, and deep around the issues of equity. Together, educators must be willing to be transformed so that we can empower students. Together, we must form alliances that will help us move from awareness to understanding to taking action in our classrooms. Using provocative texts and a variety of protocols is one way to hold ourselves accountable to each other and accountable for the success of our students.

Camilla Greene
Professional Developer, New Jersey Coalition of Essential Schools

Looking at Student Work with Colleagues

A quick skim of their papers showed me how far from the mark my students were in their thinking and understanding. I dreaded trying to think of constructive feedback. I selected Nick's essay to share with my teacher Critical Friends Group, because it reflected the shortcomings I had seen in all of the students' papers. Using the Constructivist Tuning Protocol, I asked my critical friends to search Nick's paper for understanding, because all I could see were the gaps. I felt guilty, insisting that they find something redeeming in this vague and vapid essay. It turned out not to be all that difficult for them. I took notes as they went through several rounds of "warm" feedback, their fresh eyes finding strengths in Nick's paper that my own eyes, clouded with disappointment, had missed. Their distance from the assignment also allowed them to offer "cool" feedback on his work without the harshness that I had been feeling. Hearing the group's ideas pushed me to think beyond the strengths and weaknesses of that particular piece of work to how I could help move all of the students' learning forward.

Jessie Towbin
Teacher, Illahee Junior High School, Federal Way, Washingon

Helping Students Examine Their Own Work

My positive experiences in using protocols with colleagues raised the question: why not with students? Wouldn't young people who crave fair treatment respond positively to the fairness inherent in protocols as least as well as adults?

In the past year I have been experimenting with having middle and high school students use structured protocols to examine their work in my art and photography classes. What was primarily an effective mode of adult professional development has now become a new model for the classroom. In introducing a new assignment, for instance, I have presented students with similar work from previous classes. Using a simple protocol, students speak in turn, first describing the work and then offering interpretive observations. The benefits of using the protocol are immediately evident. Students abide by the guidelines and listen to each other, rare enough in itself. Each student seems to appreciate the equal opportunity to speak, even if it is to simply say, "Pass." The initial rounds of description provide a way especially for students to bypass the knee-jerk tendency to judge, which effectively shuts down dialogue. As they step into the role of thoughtful, respectful collaborators, the conversation seems to become theirs, and I am able to comfortably assume the role of learner among learners.

Eric Baylin
Teacher, Packer Collegiate Institute, Brooklyn, New York

Refining Teaching and Learning

I work in an urban university teaching Current Issues in Elementary Urban Education, the capstone course for the elementary master's program. This puts me in the position to teach all of the master's candidates in a research and writing class as they prepare for their comprehensive exams. I do not score the comps, and therefore felt the need to bring together the professors whose questions the students answer and who score the exams. My framing question was, "What is master's level writing?" I chose the Tuning Protocol, and I presented one typical paper. Five of my colleagues engaged in the protocol and a discussion that followed. What resulted was a reformatting of the research paper to match the format professors were looking for in the comps. In addition, I completely revamped my course syllabus and broke the paper down into manageable chunks for personalized assistance. I now have regular one-on-one conferences with students wherein they bring me their work along the way. Not only have the research papers improved, the comp professors are also seeing an improvement in students' organization of their written responses on the exams.

I also use protocols with my secondary education methods students, having them work with colleagues over a quarter to "tune" their work before it is turned in to me. They get so much out of critiquing each other's work, as it gives them a different audience and valuable feedback prior to handing work in for a grade. In addition, I use protocols with my student teachers. They meet two times during a quarter and bring two lesson plans they have taught and the resulting student work. We use Collaborative Assessment Conference and end by focusing on the construction of the lesson, what happened, and how the resulting work might be improved—all helpful—and students feel very powerful.

Juli P. Quinn
Assistant Professor, California State University at Los Angeles

Preface

In 1991, a learning tool called the Tuning Protocol was introduced in a hotel conference room in Boston. This was the first time the word *protocol* was used in quite the way we use it throughout this book. The meeting's participants included educators from five urban high schools that had been funded by the IBM Corporation to devise systems for graduating students on the basis of student exhibitions. The idea was to "plan backward" from a vision of what they wanted all their graduates to know and be able to do, rethinking all their systems accordingly (McDonald, 1996; McDonald, Barton, Smith, Turner, & Finney, 1993). The participants also included a couple of high school students, executives from IBM, and staff from the Coalition of Essential Schools. The latter had organized the meeting with three purposes in mind: to introduce the educators to each other (the schools were in different regions of the country), to offer IBM an early progress report on the work it had funded, and to engage in what the organizers called "tuning." The metaphor sometimes gets a musical interpretation—as in *tuning up* the instruments—and sometimes an electromagnetic one—as in *tuning to* a different frequency. Drawing on both meanings, the organizers hoped that educators might gain new sources of insight and energy for their work by sharing honest accounts of it with each other, by giving and receiving honest feedback, and by coming to appreciate a different perspective on their joint concerns.

The organizers knew that educators are not used to "tuning," and that accomplishing it at this meeting would be particularly challenging given the meeting's other two purposes. If the participants did not even know each other—never mind trust each other—and if they were to be reporting progress to still other strangers who had given them a lot of money to make progress—wouldn't they just put on a show? Moreover, might this rare opportunity to hear about early work provoke the funders to be more critical than they ought to be at such a point? The meeting presented much possibility of social danger.

To save the tuning from the danger, the organizers designed a *protocol* to guide the meeting. Why they chose this odd word to identify their design is explained in Chapter 1. Here we say only that the protocol structured the conversation that day so that everybody got time to speak and everybody got time to listen; that presenting, examining, questioning, and responding were kept in balance; and that the meeting proved optimally honest and respectful.

Still, the meeting got off to a rocky start—predictably so, given the participants' inexperience with tuning or with protocols. Initially some of the school people resisted the facilitator's efforts to limit the presentations, and to structure the conversation. They had prepared for the meeting with a show in mind—one aimed at building the funder's confidence in their capacity to deliver the student benefits they promised. Naturally, they wanted simply to do what they thought they had come to do.

However, the facilitator insisted on the protocol, though even he buckled at one point under the pressure to put it aside. His slip proved fortuitous. It occurred when he called on one of the students to answer a question—in plain violation of the protocol's rules about when presenters may speak. His intentions were good: one of the funders had asked a question about the student's own experience, and the facilitator thought that having the chance to answer the question immediately might make the student feel more comfortable. Before he could answer the question, however, a teacher interrupted: "The students are expecting the same format as the rest of us. They know that hard questions are going to be coming at them, but they want the same time to think about their answers that the rest of us get." His statement helped everyone present understand instantly the value of a protocol. The result was that the resistance abated.

Since that day in Boston, use of the Tuning Protocol has spread (Allen, 1998; Blythe, Allen, & Powell, 1999). Since then, its use has also become linked with a number of other meeting tools to which the word *protocol* is often attached (McDonald,

2001b, 2002). We describe many of these in this book. Some involve tuning—particularly the ones that help educators study their students' work together, or help them examine each other's practice. Others involve comparable levels of social danger because they challenge long-standing norms among educators to avoid exploring complex problems or discussing controversial topics. But all of the protocols featured in the book have the premise that was made explicit in Boston: whenever talk has important consequences, we deserve a chance to think through what we want to say, and an environment where what we choose to say can be heard and respected.

Meanwhile, as the use of protocols has spread from conferences and workshops to everyday settings where colleagues meet to plan and work together, it becomes possible to imagine a new kind of workplace for educators—quite different from the kind most of us have grown accustomed to. The new kind of workplace is one that we think capable of supporting what we call genuine accountability—a spirit of collective effort to teach all our students well, and to attend assiduously to the problem of leaving none behind. Readers may use this book merely as a handbook of protocols—a collection of step-by-step accounts of how to use them to study together, work on problems of practice, and explore their students' work. We hope, however, that they will also use it to join with colleagues to imagine and then create this new kind of workplace.

ORGANIZATION OF THE BOOK

Chapter 1 explains the basic ideas underlying all the rest of the book, beginning with an argument for why we educators should educate ourselves. It also makes the case for exploring student work as a crucial element in the effort to educate ourselves. Then, at greater length, it explains what protocols are and why we need them, and finally how the "facilitative leadership" they foster can help build within our institutions the new workplace we advocate.

Chapter 2 examines the work of the facilitative leader. We

apply this term, borrowed from Roger Schwarz (1994), to every educator who has occasion to lead his or her colleagues in one of the protocols we describe—whether in the context of a simple team meeting, a multiday retreat, or any format in between. Moving the emphasis of the book from rationale to practical guidance, this chapter offers advice and step-by-step activities for facilitators of protocols. Here we also introduce the format used to present all the book's protocols—beginning with some introductory material, proceeding to a note on purpose and practical details, moving through a careful description of the steps of the protocol, providing a few facilitation tips, and finishing with some variants to consider.

Chapter 3 focuses on the crucial role of outside sources in efforts to educate ourselves. It presents protocols that we educators can use to explore texts, and to draw advice from experts. These enable bifocal attention on both the sources of new insight and the issues of practice they concern.

Chapter 4 includes protocols commonly used for problem-solving, planning, and other kinds of learning on the job. These differ from the ones presented in Chapter 3 in that they support using the artifacts and experiences of our own practice as the chief resources in educating ourselves.

Chapter 5 focuses on what is undoubtedly the most well known use of protocols today, namely the exploration of student work. It presents protocols for many different kinds and degrees of exploration, including ones aimed at deeper understanding of particular students, greater awareness of a curriculum's impact, and sharper awareness of the standards guiding teaching and learning.

It is important to note that all the protocols we present in this book, however, can be used for purposes other than the ones our chapter groupings suggest. A shift of purpose takes only the right circumstances, some modification, and a facilitator's imagination and skill. Protocols can also be used for purposes that go beyond the education of educators. For example, many teachers adapt protocols for use in their own classroom teaching—a particularly beneficial off-shoot of educating ourselves.

We encourage lots of cross-use. In this regard, we follow the lead of our favorite cookbooks—the kind that not only enable "faithful replication" but also encourage improvisation, that tell the novice how to make pesto with basil, pignoli, and parmigiano, but then suggest for future reference that it could just as well be made with any green, nut, and cheese. To support such cross-use—again in the manner of good cookbooks—we provide a table of Suggested Uses in Appendix A. Moreover, abbreviated versions of all the protocols presented in this book are available on the Teachers College Press website (http://www.teacherscollegepress.com). This is for readers to download to their own computers, to print out as needed for their own quick reference—the equivalent for facilitators of the cook's notes—and to customize the "recipes" to meet their own needs. Finally, in Appendix B, we provide information about contacting some of the organizations whose work we have drawn upon in creating this book, and whom we thank in the Acknowledgments.

Before this book entered its second printing, author Nancy Mohr died unexpectedly. Deeply saddened by the loss, her co-authors are also grateful to have the record of her work here. Meanwhile, we know that her work also lives on in the practices of the many leaders she inspired and trained, and we further dedicate our book to them and to the hope they stir up. "Hope is the thing with feathers," Emily Dickinson wrote, "that flutters in the soul, and sings the tune without the words, and never stops at all."

Acknowledgments

The use of protocols in the education of educators has roots in the efforts of at least two generations of scholars and practitioners who have attempted to bring to education insights from the fields of organizational development and human relations training. We think, for example, of the work of two scholar-teachers who provided us important counsel in the last years of their lives, Don Schön and Matt Miles. More recently, David Jacobson has helped us connect our experience within the educational field to larger organizational perspectives.

Most of what we describe and advocate in this book, however, originated in the theories and practices of education itself. Among the seminal contributors, we count Patricia Carini, Peter Elbow, James Gray, Vito Perrone, and Ted Sizer. We would also like to acknowledge the work of some clever people we know who have made prodigious contributions to the efforts we report here by designing protocols, promoting their use, and reporting on them also. We thank David Allen, Daniel Baron, Tina Blythe, Simon Clements, Anthony Conelli, Kathleen Cushman, the late Faith Dunne, Paula Evans, Helen Featherstone, Ruth Mitchell, Barbara Powell, Steve Seidel, Gene Thompson-Grove, and Viv White.

Still others' important contributions, however, are sadly beyond our capacity to trace. That is because some protocols have attained the status of lore. Still, we have attempted to document the sources of protocols (formal and informal, published or not) wherever these sources can be traced. Scholarship and courtesy demand as much, but there is learning to be gained from such documentation, too. Below the surface of attribution, the reader can trace the influence of networks and institutions that encourage and support educators educating themselves in the ways we advocate.

They include national organizations like the Coalition of Essential Schools, the National School Reform Faculty, the National Writing Project, the Annenberg Institute for School Reform at Brown University, Project Zero at the Harvard School of Education, the Education Trust, and the Institute for Learning at the University of Pittsburgh. They also include many local organizations. As New Yorkers, we especially want to acknowledge the work of the Literacy Center at Lehman College, New Visions for Public Schools, the Professional Development Lab, and the Horowitz Center for Teacher Development at New York University. But many other local organizations deserve mention. They stretch from coast to coast (from the Bay Area Coalition of Equitable Schools to the Southern Maine Partnership), with too many in between to list here. Ultimately, the aim of this book is to advance the work of such networks and institutions—nationally, regionally, and locally.

Finally, with deep gratitude for the supportive contexts they have offered us as developers, explorers, describers, and promoters of protocols, we wish to acknowledge the Department of Teaching and Learning at the Steinhardt School of Education, New York University; the New York City Department of Education; and the editors of Teachers College Press.

CHAPTER 1

The Basic Ideas

In some educational organizations, protocols may at first seem foolish—their artifice an unwarranted interference in ordinary business. The more dysfunctional this business, the stronger the negative reaction may be. For example, schools or colleges mired in norms of private practice, and used to ignoring the actual impact of the practice on students' learning, may not take easily to learning with protocols. Encouraged to try them anyway, however, and pressed to see them all the way through, even reluctant participants may find something refreshing about protocols. Then, urged to reflect on the nature of this refreshment, the participants may find that the protocols help them imagine alternatives to ordinary habits of working together, learning, and leading.

Thus emerges the possibility of what we call a new workplace for educators—the kind that Peter Senge (1990) with great resonance calls a learning organization. In this chapter, we describe four basic ideas concerning the continuing professional education of educators. These basic ideas underpin all the protocols presented in Chapters 2 through 5, and all our advice concerning their use. Together, they also constitute the basis of our vision of a new workplace for educators. As we suggested in the Preface, readers can choose merely to use this book as a handbook of professional development activities, but we hope they will use it also as an invitation to help create such a workplace within their own contexts.

EDUCATING OURSELVES

The first basic idea is that we professional educators should take charge of our own learning. That is because only we can direct it toward managing the real problems of our work, and toward meeting our students' real needs. Because these problems and needs are vastly more complex than they typically appear to others, inside perspectives are crucial to understanding them (Lampert, 2001). To say that we ought to educate ourselves, therefore, means that professional development activities for educators that are designed and conducted without benefit of inside perspectives are not worth the time and money they cost. It does not mean, however, that we should cut ourselves off from outside sources of learning. On the contrary, we desperately need what outside expertise can offer. However, we cannot effectively use outside expertise except in combination with our own intimate knowledge of practice.

It is important to note the plural in the phrase *educating ourselves.* The work it describes is necessarily collective. No educator works alone, though we seem to. Yes, we make lots of private moves, and our work demands an individual capacity for spontaneity, improvisation, and good judgment. But all our efforts for better or worse are mediated by the efforts of our colleagues. What they do matters as much to the learning of our students and the running of our programs as what we do. Thus their values, standards, and methods are our business—as ours are their business—and the problems of practice are inescapably mutual ones. For this reason, we must give up our pervasive tendency to try to manage them alone.

Indeed, we may even fail to see what our actual problems of practice are unless we dare to inquire about them together. This is because so much of our knowledge of practice is tacit, and becomes subject to critique only when we reflect on it in the company of others (Schön, 1983). It is also because certain aspects of practice—as we explain below—cause us to overlook the problems that inhere in it; and it is our colleagues who are best situated to help us understand this limit on our ordinary perspective. Finally, it is because the identification and analysis of problems require certain organizational components that are often absent within educational institutions. These include norms for open and honest conversation; meeting habits that support inquiry, dialogue, and reflection; opportunities for those immersed in particular work to take direct action to improve it; and facilitative leadership capable of encouraging participation, ensuring equity, and building trust. The only way to ensure the presence of these things within our educational institutions is through collective work on the inside. No amount of external pressure can by itself manage the task, nor can any amount of solo effort.

EXPLORING STUDENT WORK

One good way for us to educate ourselves is to pause periodically in our practice to become deliberate students of our students. This is the second basic idea underpinning this book. The point is to reach a different understanding of our students than the kind we're used to, one deeper than what is required merely to keep our teaching and their learning in sync. But this demands a great shift of energy, both practical and organizational. Instead of pressing for student work flow as we usually do, judging quickly the value of the flow's direction, we must on a regular basis suspend flow, capture images of the work interrupted, study the images calmly and deliberately, and explore together what they may mean.

Along with a broad alliance of teachers, school leaders, teacher educators, and reform-minded educators with many other job titles, we often refer to this great shift of energy with the simple phrase "looking at student work" (Allen, 1998). Here, however, we acknowledge that the "looking" we advocate is simple in the deep and disciplined way that Thoreau's looking was simple at Walden Pond and Annie Dillard's at Tinker Creek. Simple but elemental. Simple but difficult.

Students' work is the text we read in order to understand our own work. It is where our moves as educators and their impact on students are most traceable (McDonald, 2001b, 2002). It is where what we know and also what we don't know become most apparent. For these reasons, our efforts to explore student work—*together*—are crucial to our efforts to revise and improve the collective work of our educational institutions. But for these reasons, too, such efforts are threatening. This is why protocols are useful.

PROTOCOL-BASED LEARNING

The third basic idea underlying this book concerns our use of the word *protocol*. It may seem at first an odd fit with our purpose. In diplomacy, protocol governs who greets whom first when the President and Prime Minister meet, and other such matters. In technology, protocols enable machines to "talk" with one another by precisely defining the language they use. In science and medicine, protocols are regimens that ensure faithful replication of an experiment or treatment; they tell the scientist or doctor to do this first, then that, and so on. And in social science, they are the scripted questions that an inter-viewer covers, or the template for an observation. But in the professional education of educators? One could argue that elaborate etiquette, communicative precision, faithful replica-tion, and scripts would prove counterproductive here. Don't we best learn from each other by just talking with each other?

No, we claim. Among educators especially, *just* talking may not be enough. The kind of talking needed to educate ourselves cannot rise spontaneously and unaided from *just* talking. It needs to be carefully planned and scaffolded.

Making Our Work Transparent

Why should educators in particular need protocols? It is because belief in the efficacy of our efforts is a principal tool of our trade. Even when our students seem resistant, it is partly our persistence in believing in the possibilities of their learning that gives them in time the faith they need to perform well. But our unconditional believing is an occupational hazard when it comes to reflecting on our own practice. That is when, as Peter Elbow (1986) argues, the educator must temper methodological belief with methodological doubt. A good way to do this, he claims, is to alternate the two. This idea was one of several important inspi-rations for the design of the Tuning Protocol, whose debut we describe in the Preface. Another was the practice of the National Writing Project (NWP) in juxtaposing in its summer workshops for teachers three risky opportunities. The first involves sharing drafts of their own writing with each other. The second involves sharing examples of their teaching of writing with each other. And the third involves learning about the teaching of writing from experts and expert texts (Lieberman & Wood, 2003). In facing up to the first two risks—and thus gaining the benefits they offer—NWP teachers become open to understanding the comparable risk of the third and thus gaining its benefit, too. Of course, teachers hear from experts all the time—for example, in professional development workshops; but they gain real benefit from such encounters only when they dare to put their own expertise at risk (McDonald, Buchanan, & Sterling, in press).

This is difficult for us educators because we must believe in ourselves as much as in our students. We must project confidence in the directions we offer, or our students lose faith in these directions. But this has its downside. It encourages us to hide the real complexities of our work from our students, and inadvertently even from ourselves. We project such confidence in the directions we set that we conceal the choices, hunches, and inescapable uncertainty and arbitrariness that underlie them. Over time, this habit can insulate us from the gaps and faults of our own expertise, and seal us off from new expertise. Dangerously for both ourselves and our students, it can also mask the real dynamics of learning.

Protocols force transparency. By specifying, for example, who speaks when and who listens when, protocols segment elements of a conversation whose boundaries otherwise blur. They make clear the crucial differences between talking and listening, between describing and judging, or between proposing and giving feedback. In the process, they call attention to the role and value of each of these in learning, and make the steps of our learning visible and replicable.

Meanwhile, absent any effort on our part to make our work more transparent, our students grow up thinking that everything in education is clearer and more certain than it actually is—for example, what to teach, how to teach it, whether the students have learned it, what to do if they haven't, how to organize the school or other institution, and how to make it effective. Then some of the students grow up to be school board members, trustees, mayors, members of Congress, even President—and in these roles, they make policy decisions based on their faulty understanding, and these policy decisions have consequences. We work among the residual effects (in our organizational structures, institutional cultures, and work routines) of nearly a century of efforts to make education as predictable (and controllable) as it seems it should be. Educators have responded to these efforts in turn by substituting harried privacy and spurious certainty for the publicly accountable authoritativeness and creative uncertainty that our work really requires (McDonald, 1992). One of the benefits of working with protocols is that they disturb the privacy and certainty by interrupting the ordinary flow of conversation. Some of them force the raising of questions, the suspension of judgment, and the withholding of response.

Enriching Learning

In our experience, teachers who participate in protocol-based learning in their own education often adapt the protocols for their teaching. This happens, we think, because teachers already organize their practice in terms of routines—ones for which protocols may substitute, and also because teachers continually use their own learning experiences as grist for their teaching plans. Recently, Nancy Mohr worked with a group of teachers from the Packer Collegiate Institute in Brooklyn, New York, who were learning to use protocols to explore their students' work. Over the course of several months, the teachers also adapted many of these protocols to use with the students themselves, and were impressed with the quality of the work that resulted. One adapted a protocol to help her students identify whether they were predominantly visual or auditory learners, and then to reflect on what this means. The students came up with powerful lists. They were first graders. Another teacher used a protocol to help his students explore their own artwork in the same way that he and his colleagues had done.

We hope that one benefit of this book will be that readers and their colleagues will not only use the protocols we describe to educate themselves, but to educate their students as well.

Thus protocols may encourage an environment for learning (by educators *and* their students) based on the theory that knowledge is socially constructed. That is, encounters with other people's understanding enable learners to gain and deepen their own understanding. It is a theory well supported by research (Bransford, Brown, & Cocking, 1999). Moreover, along with John Dewey, we believe such learning environments foster democracy as well as cognition. They encourage learners—whether they are first graders, graduate students, or colleagues in professional education—to appreciate the value of diverse ideas and deliberative communities (Glickman, 1998; Greene, 1988; Oakes & Lipton, 1999).

Like their counterparts in diplomacy, technology, science, medicine, and social science, the kind of protocols we describe and promote in this book constrain behavior in order to enhance experience. Some protocols enable enemies to sit at the same table and make peace. Others enable scientific advancements and medical cures. Still others ensure reliable data collection and valid inference. The ones we write about help enrich educators' descriptive powers, intensify their listening, enhance their qualities of judgment, and facilitate their communication with each other. They help us to become genuinely professional and genuinely accountable.

A NEW WORKPLACE FOR EDUCATORS

The fourth basic idea informing this book concerns the consequences of taking the other ideas seriously—of educating ourselves, exploring student work together, and gaining experience in the facilitation of protocols. These can lead, we believe, to the development of what we call a new workplace for educators. This is one where the power to assess outcomes and to take action to improve them is distributed throughout the organization, and where the people who do the work are able, willing, and even eager—in consultation with their colleagues—to make changes as needed in order to make the work more effective.

Management theorists call this a high-performance workplace

(Applebaum, Bailey, Berg, & Kalleberg, 2000; Ichniowski, Levine, Olson, & Strauss, 2000). Eileen Applebaum and her colleagues outline its components within the manufacturing sector of the economy against the backdrop of the traditional workplace:

> In traditional manufacturing plans, conceptualizing and planning what needs to be done is separated from carrying out work tasks and executing plans. . . . Most employees have little autonomy or control over work tasks and methods. Managers coordinate the gathering and processing of information . . . and then use knowledge concentrated within management ranks to make decisions based on the information they have gathered. There are few opportunities for ideas to flow upward from front-line workers. Once decisions have been made, orders are relayed back down the chain of command to the front-line workers, who carry them out. Supervisors act as monitors. . . . Workers are paid to follow orders, not to think. In this setting, time spent in training or in problem-solving meetings represents lost productivity. (pp. 101–102)

With some modification, this description fits certain sectors of traditional American education, too, especially urban schooling. Indeed, the original design of urban schooling in the United States, with its emphasis on mass production and "scientific management," was imported from manufacturing (Callahan, 1962; Tyack, 1974). Sadly, evidence of these roots may be stronger today than in recent decades, given today's heightened attention to accountability. That is because pressures to achieve greater accountability are often filtered through the century-old organizational paradigm, resulting in ever more scripted curriculum, ever closer monitoring, and ultimately spurious accountability.

The lesson from the 1990s turnaround in American manufacturing, however, is that higher performance requires a change of organizational paradigm rather than greater dedication to the existing one. The heart of the change in manufacturing, according to Applebaum and her colleagues (2000), has been to reorganize work "to permit front-line workers to participate in decisions that alter organizational routines" (p. 7). Specifically, this has involved more front-line authority exercised in production teams; greater communication within and among the teams, between teams and managers, and between teams and experts in other parts of the organization; and participation by front-line workers in off-line problem-solving. In the manufacturing enterprises that Applebaum and her colleagues studied, these changes resulted in greater profitability and greater worker satisfaction.

The high-performance workplace shows up today also in the service sector of the American economy—at least, the high end of it. Charles Fishman (1996), for example, describes the high-performance workplace of the profitable and upscale Whole Foods Supermarket chain:

> The Whole Foods culture is premised on decentralized teamwork. "The team," not the hierarchy, is the defining unit of activity. Each of the 43 stores is an autonomous profit center composed of an average of 10 self-managed teams—produce, grocery, prepared foods, and so on—with designated leaders and clear performance targets. The team leaders in each store are a team; store leaders in each region are a team; the company's six regional presidents are a team. Whole Foods supports teamwork with a wide-open financial system. It collects and distributes information to an extent that would be unimaginable almost anywhere else. Sensitive figures on store sales, team sales, profit margins, even salaries, are available to every person in every location. In fact, the company shares so much information so widely that the SEC has designated all 6,500 employees "insiders" for stock-trading purposes. (p. 103)

Of course, measures of success in education are different than in steel or apparel manufacturing, or in the retailing of natural foods; and the kinds of information that people need to work smartly in schools and colleges and other educational organizations are different, too. Still, it seems plausible that some workplace innovations in manufacturing and high-end service may also work well in our field. These may especially include the use of teams—both "front-line" (to do the work), and "off-line" (to study ways to improve the work); richer information systems and far broader access to them; and the cultivation of a commitment to the organization's mission at all levels, purchased by the decentralization of management authority and accountability.

Some recent studies of school reform bear this out. Here the high-performance workplace has been associated with the development of what are called professional communities of practice. Reporting on a 4-year study of 16 high schools in two states, for example, Milbrey McLaughlin and Joan Talbert

(2001) depict a subsample of schools that consistently engaged diverse students in challenging academic work, and kept them engaged and successful over time. These schools were notable for the presence of a "strong professional community committed to making innovations that support student and teacher learning and success"(pp. 38–39). Similarly, Fred Newmann and Gary Wehlage (1995), reporting on a national study of 24 restructured schools, conclude that "the most successful schools were the ones that used restructuring tools to help them function as professional communities of practice" (p. 3). Where such communities had the right cultural and structural conditions to exert continual leadership, the researchers say, and where they focused on improving the intellectual quality of their students' work, the work did improve (Newmann & Associates, 1996; Newmann & Wehlage, 1995).

In a recent national survey of American public school teachers, 69% reported a higher amount of collaboration in their work life than 3 years before, with 36% reporting a "lot more" collaboration (Belden Russonello & Stewart Research and Communications, 2000). Still, the presence of professional communities of practice in American schooling seems far from the norm. Indeed, the same survey suggests that the decline in front-line privacy reported by teachers has been accompanied by increased rather than decreased bureaucratic constraints on their work, especially in the form of testing requirements.

Meanwhile, many calls for accountability in education and plans for achieving it continue to take little account of the gap between aspiration and organizational reality. For example, some reformers argue that malfunctioning urban school systems can be redirected toward student achievement by turning them over to "accountable" mayors (Kirst, 2002). Cities now implementing this "reform" include New York City, Boston, Chicago, Cleveland, and Detroit (Gewertz, 2002). It is as if accountability were a kind of fluid that could be squeezed through an educational organization starting from the top, and as if the organization were a kind of vacuum of accountability to begin with.

We think differently. For one thing, we know that the status quo is not an accountability vacuum but a different (though inadequate) kind of accountability system based on different assumptions about the goals of education (Abelmann & Elmore, 1999). These are rooted in policy-making focused on controlling how every job is done, rather than on building capacity for doing the real job well (Darling-Hammond, 1998). Doing the real job well involves unlearning the controls, and substituting an accountability based on faithfulness to learning. This is one that combines front-line scrutiny of student work, collective responsiveness to individual student needs, and strategic flexibility at all levels of the organization. In this way the smallest units of the organization become the source of its cohesion overall, as Margaret Wheatley (2000) explains:

> If the organization can stay in a continuous conversation about what it is and what it is becoming, then leaders don't have to undertake the impossible task of trying to hold it all together. Organizations that are clear at their core hold themselves together because of their deep congruence. (p. 343)

The best way to be clear at the core, we think, is to build professional communities of practice (McLaughlin & Talbert, 2001). This is where educators can learn and unlearn whatever scrutiny, responsiveness, and strategic flexibility require. This is where they can educate themselves accordingly. Such education is usually needed, since no education preset in its purposes—whether offered in outside courses and workshops or "in-service" ones—can fully meet the needs of professionals really attentive to their own students and their own contexts. Professional communities of practice inevitably need learning that only its own members can supply.

FACILITATIVE LEADERSHIP

Karen Seashore Louis and her colleagues (1996) argue that the crucial components of professional communities of practice are the following:

- Focus on student learning
- Deprivatization of practice

- Collaboration
- Shared norms and values
- Reflective dialogue

The first two of these require difficult shifts in organizational values and structures. By and large, most educational organizations today are focused more on their own smooth running than on student learning, and this smooth running depends in large measure on keeping practice private and serious talk about practice minimal. Some reformers aim to improve matters quickly by pressing directly for a focus on student learning and/or the deprivatization of practice, while paying insufficient attention to the rest of the items on the researchers' list. These reformers may insist, for example, on accountability with respect to certain indicators of student learning such as test scores, but neglect the problem of how educators used to working alone and ignoring such indicators might suddenly reverse emphasis. Or they may insist on educators working in teams, but provide no models or coaching. Or they may provide time for educators to meet together for planning, but no norms for planning or frameworks of values to guide it.

We argue that all the elements on the list are crucial, and that efforts to achieve a new and more genuinely accountable workplace for educators must work simultaneously to cultivate them all. We argue further that a good way to do this is to invest systematically in the development of distributed facilitative leadership. This means working to ensure that there are people throughout the organization who know how to do the following (Schwarz, 1994):

- Gather colleagues together with a purpose
- Establish effective ground rules for the gatherings
- Enforce the ground rules by identifying behaviors consistent and inconsistent with them
- Enable the colleagues to share information freely with each other
- Help them attend fully to each other's perspectives
- Help them make a collective commitment to the choices the group may make

When we use the word *facilitator* in this book, we mean someone empowered by role or opportunity to do these things. In an educational organization, this someone may be a workshop or task force leader; a member of a teaching team; the principal, dean, or other administrator; the chair of a standing committee; a parent or student leader; or any staff member suddenly called upon on an ad hoc basis to organize others to learn together, improve practice, solve problems, or develop action plans. Of course, the facilitator may also be an outside consultant. However, over time—and partly as a result of the thoughtful use of outside consultants—enough insiders can become good facilitators that outsiders are needed only in special circumstances. This is when the organizations may be said to have developed facilitative leadership.

One of the values of using protocols as learning formats, in our view, is that they can accelerate the development of facilitative leadership, and thus assist in the creation of new workplaces for educators. This is because in some important respects they make the tasks of facilitation more transparent. Of course, facilitators of protocols still have to make many important on-the-job calls: how to strike and keep a balance between comfort and alertness, whether to speed up the pace or slow it down, how to press for honesty but also soften its occasionally hard impact, and so on. On the other hand, they do not have to make many other calls—for example, who talks when and for how long, and even what they talk about. That is because many protocols preset these. Moreover—at least as we promote the role and the task—facilitators of protocols do not decide the purposes of the learning they facilitate, nor judge its ultimate effects. Our claim that we professional educators need to educate ourselves means especially that these decisions need to be collectively made.

Thus freed from some kinds of decision-making, facilitators of protocols have more energy for making the decisions they must, and for reflecting on the results. Such experience over time can make them good facilitators of other meeting formats besides protocol-based ones, and thus deepen their organization's overall capacity with respect to facilitative leadership.

In the next chapter, we examine more deeply the facilitator's role, and offer practical advice to facilitators—including some protocols they may use to manage some parts of their role. Here we say merely—and in conclusion—that this role may be more powerful than it usually seems; that those good at managing the "process" of educational reform may, in the end, control the fate of its "content"; and that the more an educational organization cultivates people who can play this role well, the healthier it may become.

CHAPTER 2

Facilitating

At its heart, facilitating is about promoting participation, ensuring equity, and building trust. This is true whether the facilitating involves a protocol or another kind of meeting format. The difference is that protocols are deliberately designed with these tasks in mind, while most other meeting formats are rife with opportunities for ignoring them. We all know the result: the faculty "meeting" that turns into a monologue by the principal or the chairperson, the "discussion" that two or three people dominate, or the task force that manages to suppress dissent.

Of course, protocols are no panacea for these or any other kinds of collegial problems, but they are valuable in highlighting the fact that the problems exist. In offering colleagues the image of an alternative reality, they may also encourage efforts to address the problems. Thus someone might say, "Let's have more of the kind of faculty meetings we had that one time, when everyone got a chance to talk, and everybody's ideas got heard and responded to."

To promote participation, ensure equity, and promote trust, the facilitator needs, first of all, an "appointment." It may be a formal one—as in the announcement that "George will lead the task force," or it may be informal, as in a colleague's asking, "Hey, George, why don't you facilitate the group this time?" In either case, George also has to have a full understanding of what the appointment entails. He has to understand that the three tasks—involving participation, equity, and trust—are at the heart of the work he is being asked to do. Furthermore, he must be willing and able to perform the tasks. One aim of this book is to help spread such understanding, willingness, and ability throughout educational organizations. This is crucial, we think, to the effort to make them workplaces that are genuinely accountable.

THE FACILITATOR'S CORE TASKS

One reason why competent facilitators are in short supply today, however, is that many organizational environments discount the importance of the facilitator's core tasks. The facilitator deals merely with "process," some like to say, but what really matters is "content": "getting the information across," "accomplishing the task," "making the decision." We believe, however, that "content" has a way of evaporating in the absence of participation, equity, and trust.

For this reason, we begin our practical advice about facilitating by offering some arguments about why encouraging participation, ensuring equity, and building trust matter so much—and how they relate to content. With such arguments to rely on, the facilitator need not fear the old accusation that he or she is being "touchy-feely."

Promoting Participation

Learning is social. We inevitably learn through and with others, even though what is finally understood is our own mental construction (Bransford, Brown, & Cocking, 1999). In insisting that educators learning together get to know each other first, the facilitator is not just encouraging cordiality. Openness to others' experiences builds openness to others' perspectives, and such openness provides learning opportunities otherwise unavailable.

When the facilitator encourages participants in a protocol to "hear all voices," it is really a call to highlight a sufficient number of perspectives on the issue or problem at hand such that everyone can gain the possibility of new insight. It is also a call to pool knowledge and thus become smarter in the aggregate, to cultivate and rely upon what Lauren Resnick (1987) calls shared cognition, which she properly distinguishes as the hallmark of most complex work situations outside education. Finally, it is a call to suspend what our friend Paul Naso calls the ordinary political cross-currents of schools and colleges—the ones that may cause the newer people to hold their tongues while the veterans speak, that may give some people used to exerting influence more than their due share of it, and that may perpetuate old culture within new structures.

Ensuring Equity

The presumption of a genuinely accountable educational organization is that everyone can learn what he or she needs to learn in order to do the work at hand. This *everyone* involves adults as well as students. The difficulty in living up to such a presumption comes from the fact that people learn in different ways, including ways that may seem aberrant: the child who persists in walking around or talking out of turn; the adult who talks too much or too little, or who seems always to disagree or to digress.

In striving for the inclusion of such people, the facilitator does more than protect their opportunities for learning, or smooth out social ripples. He or she also implicitly acknowledges the value of difference in the group's learning, and helps the group strive to understand the contribution it may make. In doing so, the facilitator makes room for dissidence, and may even stretch colleagues' capacity for learning from it. A norm that respects dissidence is crucial to genuine accountabiliy. Until a professional community really knows and understands the range of viewpoints it contains—however variable and contradictory—it remains incapable of taking collective and effective action on behalf of all its students' learning. That is because it ends up screening out—for the sake of its own false consensus—exactly the differences it needs to consider.

Building Trust

Educators educating themselves rely on each other's honesty, insight, and experience. Going public with their work, they let each other in on what they are doing, thinking, learning, and hoping. They invite one another's perspectives in the expectation that these will be valuable. They invite the collective experience of the group to serve as the arbiter of their own growth. All of these efforts require a trustful situation.

It is important to consider, however, what a trustful situation really is and what it is for. It is situational. When a facilitator promotes a group's trust, it is not to help everyone trust every other individual member *as an individual,* but rather to help each trust the situation that has been collectively created. The purpose is not trust in general, but trust sufficient to do the work at hand. Nor is the goal to make everyone feel comfortable. Given trust, a group of individuals can learn from each other and their work together even when the work creates *dis*comfort—as work involving worthwhile learning often does.

THE FACILITATOR'S MOVES

Facilitating protocols involves long-term planning—as in what protocol to use when, and how to open and close the meeting—and also judgments made in the moment—as in how to intervene when something goes wrong, and when to change one's plan. In what follows, we offer some advice about some of the better moves to use at these and other points, and how to use them.

Opening

Sometimes facilitators who use protocols think the people they work with won't need any warm-up. "Well," they say, "I think I'll just start with looking at students' work [or dealing with controversial topics, or planning collaboratively] and skip all of that 'touchy-feely' stuff." In the process, as we suggest above, they may undercut their purpose. Preparing educators to give and get sensitive feedback is not a lightweight distraction or lure. It is the developmentally crucial start of building a professional learning environment. No one can give and get feedback sensitively, honestly, and effectively without first knowing a little bit about everybody else involved, discussing the context in which they are gathered—or what is often called the agenda—and setting or reviewing some group norms.

Sometimes, facilitators who understand the value of opening

moves are nonetheless tempted to skip them because they think there is not enough time. Time is always an issue in the facilitation of groups. In our experience, however, a little investment of time up front saves a lot of time later.

What matters most in the selection of an opening move is that the one selected seem relevant to the business at hand. Disconnected openers provoke the "touchy-feely" accusation, and seem as incongruous as an off-color joke at the start of a serious speech. It matters, too, that the scale of the opening move fit the scale of the meeting: short moves for short time-frames; longer ones for half-day sessions or day-long retreats.

In whatever form they take, however, the opening moves that should never be skipped are introductions, context review, and norm-setting. This is true for any group meeting, including ones governed by protocols.

Introductions have two general purposes. The first is to get everybody present to say something right away—something that connects each to the business of the group. People who speak early at a meeting are more likely to avoid the prolonged silence that might otherwise envelop them and become a source of tension for themselves as well as others. The second purpose is to help everyone know something relevant about each of the people now joining them in a learning activity, and thus representing in a symbolic way the presence of a distributed intelligence and of its usefulness to the group's learning purpose.

Context review includes what we plan to work on and why, how we came to be here, what we hope to achieve, and how long and in what ways we plan to work together. A protocol usually defines only the last of these; the others need to be explained, discussed, perhaps negotiated.

Norms are not the rules set down in the protocol, though these are also crucial to explain. Norms are behavioral guidelines whose purpose goes beyond the meeting itself. They signify ways of being together and learning from each other that we hope will become habitual. For example, they help participants come to view discomfort not as an avoidable aberration but as a necessary part of the learning process. They involve such other things as how we treat each other's ideas and how we push our own thinking. They also involve things such as whether we talk about what has transpired within the meeting outside the meeting, whether we turn off cell phones during the meeting, and how we expect our facilitator to work with us.

Intervening and Closing

Even though protocols help prevent things from going wrong (by providing an overarching structure that participants can trust), unexpected things still happen that require intervention. Once one of us was facilitating a protocol in a room where two or three nonparticipants were at the periphery working at computers. Speaking within the parameters of the protocol, one participant began to speak about race, whereupon someone at the periphery interrupted. The facilitator explained to the person that the group was using a constrained form of conversation, and that if he wanted to join the conversation, he would have to sit at the table and follow the protocol, too. He declined to get involved. Later, however, he interrupted again. At that point, the facilitator ought to have asked him to leave the room—or, alternatively, moved the protocol to a more private space. Instead, the facilitator permitted the person to enter the conversation on his own terms, and effectively gave up facilitating the protocol. Later, the participant whose contribution had been interrupted told the facilitator that she had felt deserted by the one person she had expected to keep the difficult conversation safe. It was clearly a bad move on the facilitator's part.

Situations demanding facilitator interventions are usually somewhat easier to handle than this. For example, a participant new to the protocol format might momentarily lose the suspension of disbelief that new participants usually need, and might say something like: "This is silly. Why don't we just talk?" Generally, a confident admonition to trust the process a little longer, combined with a reminder that we will debrief the process in the end, is enough to quell the uprising.

Some protocols—for example, the New York Peer Review Protocol described in Chapter 5—encourage the facilitator to help regulate the conversation by participating in it substantively—for example, offering a supportive comment to the presenter to offset a string of critical ones, or pressing for more

attention to the criteria for reviewing student work. Other protocols, however, discourage this kind of substantive involvement by the facilitator. In such cases, problems that really need
intervention require either brief interruptions or longer time-
outs. During a time-out, it is better to engage in some silent
activity to help participants gather their thoughts about whatever has provoked the intervention before asking them to discuss it. Merely taking a 10-minute break can also be a useful
intervention.

Intervening moves try to preserve or revise the learning process,
while closing moves try to ensure the learning itself carries over into
the educators' ordinary work life. The latter is best achieved
through meta-cognition. That is, participants must take the trouble
to specify what they have learned—substantively and procedural-
ly—and then to generalize from it. One way the facilitator can help
with this transfer is to press participants to answer three questions,
ones that are useful to nearly any kind of debriefing:

- *What?* What have I learned about the topic that brought this
  group together?
- *So what?* What difference does it seem to make—for example,
  to my teaching or my team's planning?
- *Now what?* What steps can I take to make the most of what I
  have learned?

These questions require some time for private consideration
and for public discussion—though not necessarily much time.
When it comes to closing especially, short moves often work best.

BRIEF PROTOCOLS

Sometimes it is best to open or close a protocol-based meeting
with the use of another, briefer protocol—or even to intervene
with a briefer protocol-within-a-protocol. This is especially true
when time is less of an issue—for example, at a full-morning
meeting. In what follows, we describe some brief protocols that
can be used as opening, closing, or intervening moves. Later, we
also describe three elaborate protocols that can serve as opening

moves for meetings where time is plentiful and a good start crucial—for example, a day-long or multiday retreat.

POSTCARDS

The facilitator says, "Without looking at it first, deal yourself one of the picture postcards from this deck going around. Then imagine why it's the perfect picture for you at this moment [or how it represents your work, or describes your feelings about starting or ending the workshop]. Be prepared to show and tell."

We especially like to use black-and-white "art" cards, because they lend themselves to interpretation. A variation is to have people find the person with the same card (provided there are duplicates available) and discuss their different reactions. Given a smaller supply of postcards, the facilitator might ask two or three people to share the same card.

The activity ends with a Go-Round (see below), in which everybody has a minute to share.

REFLECTION ON A WORD

This is an activity associated with Patricia Carini's Prospect Center and its work in Descriptive Review of the Child (Himley & Carini, 2000). Before beginning a Review, participants are often asked to focus on a word that the facilitator has chosen with the child in mind. In describing this use, Elaine Avidon (2000) beautifully suggests its power:

> We spoke of *enough* as a word of measure having to do with both persons and things, quantity and quality. We placed our depictions of *enough* on a continuum with notions of adequate and appropriate at its center, and too much and too little at the edges. On this continuum, *enough* was a boundary line, a standard either achieved, not yet realized, or exceeded. At issue was whose measure, whose standards, whose evaluation. (p. 36, emphasis in original)

In our adaptation of the protocol, participants introduce themselves briefly, then give their own takes on the word *literacy* (or whatever word seems relevant to the work at hand). This helps everyone see the multiple takes that a word can invoke, and establishes the norm that different takes are useful and help-ful to the group's learning overall. This activity can also be a good intervention; taking a moment to clarify—or problematize—a word or term can help clear the air, or generate new insight when it may be especially needed.

PAIR-SHARE

Participants all share with a partner some past experience related to the goals of the meeting. Experiences might include a positive one they have had in a professional workshop, or best and worst experiences taking a test, or an earliest memory of being a student, or something about their first day as a principal. All pairs address the same question, then discuss as a group what their sharing had in common and what surprised them. Obviously, Pair-Share can also provide a useful intervention at times, and a good reflective close.

CLEARING

This protocol is also known as Connections. People come to meetings or leave them with things on their minds, and they need time to transition from there to here or here to there. It helps enormously to take the time, from 5 to 10 minutes, for the group members to say what things are on their minds. There are simple rules: Nothing is too irrelevant; there can be no dialogue; each person talks only once unless everyone else has spoken; and silence is okay. When time is up, gently move on or adjourn. This is an especially good starter for an after-school workshop when people come in still connected to some earlier events, or for a closing when a protocol session has been particularly intense.

ALL-PURPOSE GO-ROUND

This is perhaps the single most important protocol a facilitator can know. The prompt can be as simple as "Introduce yourself and tell us one thing you like about technology and one thing you dis-like." The facilitator can keep it simple by making sure that people don't jump in and that the time frame stays inviolate. One way to do this is to specify a time allotment—say, 30 seconds each—and to signal by using body language when the time is up: intent listening with smiling and nodding, then a nod of the head or shift of the eyes to indicate that it is the next person's turn. Turns can thus be signaled with no facilitator talking at all.

We call this protocol "All-Purpose" because one can use it not only as an opener but as a closing move, too, or as an intervening one. Thus a facilitator can interrupt another activity to "do a quick Go-Round" of people's reactions to something that just happened, or even of whether to continue the larger activity.

LONGER OPENERS

The following long opening moves are described in the same format used to present the rest of the book's protocols. It begins by introducing the protocol, usually with a reference to its source. Next it acknowledges the particular purpose for which the protocol seems designed. Then it notes important details such as time frame and any materials or special settings required. Next it lays out the steps of the protocol. Whenever we believe that including a time frame for a step will help users understand the step better, we include one. Often, however, we leave timing for steps to facilitator discretion. Finally, the format includes some facilitation tips and some possibilities for variation.

FEARS AND HOPES

We have seen versions of this protocol used to open many kinds of meetings in many different places. Its effectiveness depends on the fact that people rarely undertake a new learning experience without harboring some (usually unexpressed) fears and hopes about what will happen. This protocol gets these into the open.

Some facilitators hesitate to open with a "negative" question such as "What are your fears about this meeting?" Their own fear is that the negativity will get out of hand. However, our experience is quite the opposite. When participants are encouraged to say aloud that they fear the meeting will be boring, will not meet their real needs, or will be run in a way that is insulting to their learning, then they become, paradoxically, much more open and receptive to the work of the actual meeting. Having accepted this first risk, they feel less defensive about others that may come their way.

Purpose

One purpose is simply to help people learn some things about each other. But the deeper purpose is to establish a norm of ownership by the group of every individual's expectations and concerns—to get these into the open, and to begin addressing them together.

Details

Time for this protocol can vary from 5 to 25 minutes, depending on the size of the group and the range of their concerns. If the group is particularly large, the facilitator asks table groups to work together and then report out. The only supplies needed are individual writing materials, newsprint, and markers.

Steps

1. *Introduction.* The facilitator asks participants to write down briefly for themselves their greatest fear for this meeting/workshop/retreat/year: "If it's the worst experience you've had, what will have happened (or not happened)?" Then they write their greatest hope: "If this is the best meeting you've ever attended, what will be its outcome(s)?"

2. *Pair-share.* If time permits, the facilitator asks participants to share their hopes and fears with a partner.

3. *Listing.* Participants call out fears and hopes as the facilitator lists them on separate pieces of newsprint.

4. *Debriefing.* The facilitator prompts, "Did you notice anything surprising or otherwise interesting while doing this activity? What was the impact on you or others of expressing negative thoughts? Would you use this activity in your school? In your classroom? Why? Why not?"

Facilitation Tips

The facilitator should list all fears and hopes exactly as expressed, without editing, comment, or judgment. One should not be afraid of the worst fears. A meeting always goes better once these are expressed. The facilitator can also participate by listing his or her own fears and hopes. After the lists of fears and hopes are complete, the group should be encouraged to ponder them. If some things seem to need modification, the facilitator should say so in the interest of transparency, and make the modifications. If some of the hopes seem to require a common effort to realize, or if some of the fears require a special effort to avoid, the facilitator should say what he or she thinks these are, and solicit ideas for generating such efforts. It is easy to move from here into norm-setting: "In order to reach our hoped-for outcomes while making sure we deal with our fears, what norms will we need?"

Variation

One variation that cuts down on time is to use pictures or picture postcards that have fairly ambiguous meaning, and to ask participants to introduce themselves and tell how the images they have picked (randomly) express their hopes or fears for the meeting. In this variation, the facilitator listens carefully and makes notes while participants speak, so as to be able to capture expressed hopes and fears for the group's reflection.

PROTOCOL FOR SETTING NORMS

Sometimes facilitators follow Fears and Hopes with this protocol, saying something like, "What norms do we need to increase the likelihood that our hopes will be realized and our fears allayed?" Nancy Mohr learned this protocol from Fran Vandiver, a former Florida principal. They were together in a school coaches' training that wasn't going well. Fran suggested that the group set norms, and Nancy thought at first that this was a terrible idea. "After all," she said to herself, "everyone here is an adult." This is a common naïve assumption, akin to "Why can't we start off with a long lecture? After all, everyone chose to learn about this topic," or "Why can't we just have a conversation about this controversy or conflict? I'm sure everyone will have something constructive to say."

Purpose

We set norms first of all to curtail some unproductive behaviors (for example, "Don't monopolize the airtime"). We also set them to give ourselves permission to be bolder than we might otherwise be (for example, "Take some risks here"). And we set them in order to remind ourselves that people learn in different ways (for example, "Give everybody time to think"). Norms are especially useful when newcomers are likely to arrive after the work is already under way (and this happens frequently in professional learning groups). When newcomers arrive, the norms fill them in. They don't have to learn them through trial and error. Norms are also useful when "tricky" conversations are likely (and tricky conversations are frequent in real-life groups).

Details

Norm-setting can take 10 minutes or much longer. Once a group that Nancy Mohr was facilitating took an hour to decide whether airtime should be restricted. The vociferous objections to this proposed norm came from a group of men used to dominating meetings they attend. But the norm was set despite their objection, and later one of them confessed publicly how much he had learned from listening for a change.

Steps

1. *Brainstorming.* The facilitator encourages the group to brainstorm all possible norms, and lists the offerings on chart paper. But the process begins with a few moments of silence as people consider what they want to offer. The facilitator also participates

in the brainstorming, adding whatever seems lacking for the emerging list—for example, "We want to create a place that is safe enough in order for us to endure discomfort," or "We want to be allowed to take a risk."

2. *Discussion.* The facilitator says, "So far this is just a brainstormed list—we have not yet agreed to it. Is there something which needs discussion, which you want to question?"

3. *Synthesis.* In a transparent way—that is, voicing his or her deliberations aloud—the facilitator synthesizes and fine-tunes: "I think that what I'm hearing is that we want to be assured that good judgment will prevail. There can be situations where a phone must be left on, and we don't want to prevent that when needed. On the other hand, we don't want a bunch of phones ringing. So maybe the norm should be that we will only leave phones on when our judgment tells us we must. This is good. I was going to just say 'No phones,' but this is much better."

4. *Consensus.* Noting that consensus means that all group members can live with and support the norms, the facilitator moves the group to affirm the list.

Facilitation Tips

The facilitator should point out to the group that we call these things "norms" because they are not "rules." Norms require flexibility yet provide guidance. Moreover, norms can be changed at any time. Indeed, norms that are intended to serve the group over a period of time are useful only if they are revisited with some regularity. Therefore, it is good to reflect on them from time to time: "How are we doing with our norms?" Meanwhile, for groups that meet over time, the chart paper with the norms can be carried over from meeting to meeting. Reviewing how the norms worked can be a good closing activity.

Variation

When time is really short the facilitator can provide a list of norms for the group's consideration. Two excellent facilitators we know, Daniel Baron and Gene Thompson-Grove, both of the National School Reform Faculty, sometimes say: "There is only one norm: If you think it, say it. If you wonder it, ask it."

Diversity Rounds

Nancy Mohr and Judith Scott had been working with a group of secondary school teachers in Indiana, exploring the principles of the Coalition of Essential Schools. Having worked with this same group for quite some time, they realized that it was time to challenge the group a bit, especially around issues related to diversity and equity. They developed this activity as a means of stimulating a conversation.

In each round, members of the group subdivided according to a particular "identifier" called out by Mohr or Scott: first the subject they taught, then where they grew up, and next their gender. Following each round, members of the subgroups discussed the impact on their professional lives of the particular identifier. Nancy remembers that the men stood around perplexed and fairly silent when it came time to discuss the impact of their gender on their professional lives. Not so the women.

Then, in the final round, the group of 80 teachers regrouped by "race." There was something of a gasp as the 79 White teachers went to one side of the room and the lone Black teacher to the other. In the process of debriefing the activity, the White people said how much fun the early rounds had been, and how uncomfortable the last. The Black teacher, however, expressed her appreciation. The discomfort for her had surfaced long before the final round, when she recognized that apart from one of the cofacilitators, she was the only Black person present. Acknowledging this fact actually helped.

Purpose

To help participants become more aware of the various connections they have to others, and to understand the impact of personal identity on professional experience. The activity is most useful for groups that will be working together over an extended time.

Details

Especially effective with large groups, Diversity Rounds can be undertaken with almost any group of more than 20 members.

The space must allow for people to move around. This activity is best done standing the entire time.

Steps

1. *Introduction.* The facilitator explains that the participants will be asked to group and then regroup themselves three to five times, according to certain identity criteria, and that they will be moving about as they do this. The facilitator explains that the identities are purposefully vague, and that participants will have to define them in their own way. Once in a particular grouping, participants will talk about how the group's identity has shaped them as professionals.

2. *Grouping.* The facilitator asks participants to find people who are from the same group as they. For example, "Find people who come from the same place as you do." Typically people need encouragement to get moving. After they have formed groups, the facilitator reminds them to introduce themselves to each other and talk about how "coming from that area" has had an impact on them as professionals. (5–10 minutes, depending on the size of the group)

3. *Reporting.* The facilitator gives a 1-minute warning, then asks groups to report out a little of what they discussed. (5 minutes)

4. *Regrouping.* After each group reports, the facilitator asks people to regroup by another category, and repeat the steps. For example: "Now regroup by place in your family." Other possible groupings: kind of high school you attended, decade of your birth, gender, race, family size, many others.

5. *Debriefing.* The facilitator should ask participants how they felt during the activity, and also how their feelings may have changed from one grouping to the next. He or she should also ask them what they have learned about diversity, and about how diversity affects professional experience.

Facilitation Tips

Getting participants to move for the first round is the most difficult. The facilitator should push hard for this. Past that, everyone begins to have fun. The laughter that develops as groups form and re-form signifies identity. One way to help participants appreciate the connection between identity and diversity—which Beverly Daniel Tatum (1992, 1999) explores well—is to press them to notice this laughter and to theorize about its causes.

It is important to do several rounds of relatively unthreatening categories of difference before attempting an uncomfortable one—where there is plainly a history of discrimination and possibly of personal hurt—for example, race, gender, ethnic identity, or age. It is important also to be sensitive in debriefing a round that does take account of any of these differences.

The prompts for regrouping need not be very clear-cut. For example, the one we mention above—"place in your family"—is likely to initially puzzle people. Is it about birth order? But what about people who have no siblings, or were foster children or stepchildren, or who were adopted? Sensing such puzzlement and finding a way through it can be a powerful outcome of the activity. The facilitator should discourage "correct answers" to the questions raised. "Birth order groupings work," he or she says, "but other kinds of groupings might, too. It depends on the diversity of the group."

Like all protocols, whether openers or not, this one needs a purpose, and the purpose needs to be kept in mind. Is it just about helping the group appreciate the fact that it is, like most other groups, diverse in important ways? If so, three rounds are probably enough. On the other hand, if there are particular issues related to diversity that the group needs to explore, then more rounds may be needed. The facilitator should work at the edge of his or her comfort zone with regard to the basis of the groupings, but also be prepared to change plans depending on how things go.

Variation

A version of Diversity Rounds can be used to explore organizational identity and diversity. For example, "Group yourselves by department [or grade level, or research interests].

Now talk about how this identification affects your work. . . . Okay, now group yourself by the course [or subject, or age] you most often teach."

MARVIN'S MODEL

We learned this years ago from a professor at a Midwestern university who used it routinely in his classes. All we can remember now is his first name, which has stuck to the protocol in the many contexts where it is now used.

Purpose

To facilitate rapid communication about a topic at hand among a large group of people, or to get many points of view quickly in play without engaging in dialogue. This can be used to open or close a meeting, or on occasion to intervene.

Steps

1. *Introduction.* The facilitator asks the large group to break into subgroups of five to seven members, then instructs the subgroups as follows: "When I ask a question, I will give you 30 seconds to think, and then each member of your group will answer quickly, in turn. Each will get exactly 30 seconds to answer. As each member speaks, the others listen silently. No one responds to anyone else's answer."

2. *Questions.* The facilitator poses a series of questions, for example, "What's the first thing you think about when I say *mathematics* [or *writing*, or *science*]?" "What do you think about when it comes to the *teaching* of mathematics [writing, science]?" "How about the *assessment* of learning in mathematics [writing, science]?"

3. *Debriefing.* Following several questions, the facilitator debriefs the group: "What has the group learned from this first exploration of the topic at hand? What, if anything, do members think we might have to unlearn?"

Facilitation Tips

Some participants will be unable to form an answer to some questions in the time provided. The facilitator should allow for this, granting permission to take a pass. Later, the facilitator can point out that both the answers and the passes may provide insight for the debriefing.

Variations

Besides being used as an opener, Marvin's Model can be used as a way of generating spontaneous responses to a speaker or a reading, responses that can then be followed up in a discussion. It can also be used in closing, as a way to share a lot of complex reaction in a relatively short amount of time.

CHAPTER 3

Tapping Outside Sources

Responsible direction of our own education as professional educators necessarily involves consulting with many others. They may not know as much as we about the intricacies and intimacies of our educational practice—which is why we need to oversee our own learning—but they know other things that are crucial for us. These may involve the subjects we teach, the development of learners (including us), theories of change and theories of organization, and much more.

We teach the world, but the world and theories about the world continually change. We need to pay attention to the changes. Moreover, attending to the views of outsiders also enables us to stay politically astute, and this is very important, since education is always at its heart political.

The protocols we feature in this chapter focus on outside sources of information and insight, and also on the problems associated with accessing these sources, understanding them, and adjusting our practices accordingly.

FINAL WORD

This is a very versatile protocol developed by Daniel Baron and Patricia Averette for the National School Reform Faculty. It is useful in exploring any kind of text, including controversial ones. For example, in a graduate preservice teacher education course, Beth McDonald uses it to explore some texts concerning racial identity—a crucial topic in the course, but a risky one, too. Neither the texts that Beth uses nor the topic itself lend themselves easily to open discussion. (Indeed, in our experience, few good texts or topics do.) In most open discussions, some students dominate, others retreat into silence, and important viewpoints are invariably lost or undervalued.

Students come to Beth's class having read Peggy McIntosh's (1989) essay "White Privilege: Unpacking the Invisible Knapsack," and also Beverly Tatum's (1992) powerful piece about racial identity. Beth then arranges the class into groups of three students each and follows the steps outlined below, managing the time herself by calling out the switches, rather than relying on the group's own timekeeping. She tells her students that the timing will be "rigid for a purpose," but that they will have more relaxed time later to talk about whatever the timing may squeeze out. The version presented here is one developed and favored by Beth.

Purpose

The purpose of the Final Word Protocol is to expand the interpretation of one or more texts by encouraging the emergence of a variety of interests, viewpoints, and voices. By forcing everyone to offer an interpretation, and to listen closely to and reflect back others' interpretations, Final Word ensures the emergence of diverse perspectives on texts. It also helps participants feel safer in proposing what may be offbeat or dissident interpretations because the protocol implicitly avoids consensus-building. It is okay in this protocol to end a session with as much difference of interpretation in the air as was there at the start. The point is to get it in the air.

Details

Final Word generally takes from 30 to 60 minutes (depending on group size) and is best done in groups of three to six. It works especially well when the facilitator wants a large group to engage with the same text and breaks it into smaller groups. Participants must have copies of the text(s). Texts may have been read in advance, or they may be read on the spot (though then they must be short, and the facilitator must allow for varied reading times and for a bit of mulling over). A watch with a countdown alarm or some other timer can be a very helpful tool for this and other protocols with tight time lines.

Steps

1. *Introduction and selection.* The facilitator introduces the whole protocol, providing copies of a short list of the steps involved. Then he or she asks all participants to select from one of the texts a short passage that has particular meaning for them, a meaning they would like to call attention to.

2. *Arrangement.* The whole group breaks into tight circles of three to six participants each. The facilitator assigns an order of presentation for participants in each circle—for example, "The person in your group whose back is most turned to the door is number one, and the person to his right is number two, etc." Each circle is asked to assign a strict timekeeper within each group. Alternatively, the facilitator can serve as timekeeper for the entire room, calling out the time switches.

3. *Presentation.* Presenter number one presents the passage he or she has identified, reading aloud and having people follow along on their copies. The presenter speaks for 2 or 3 uninterrupted minutes about it (with the timing clear in advance).

4. *Reflecting back.* Each listener in turn has 1 uninterrupted minute to "reflect back" on what the presenter has said. The facilitator has explained that reflecting back means exploring the presenter's interpretation of the passage, not adding one's own interpretation. A listener might begin, "From what you said, I can see that you are concerned about . . . ."

5. *Final word.* The round ends with a 1-minute uninterrupted time for the presenter to react to what has just been said.

6. *Round repeats.* Rounds two, three, etc. follow until all members of each group have presented and had their final word.

7. *Written reflection.* Following the rounds, the facilitator

asks everyone to write for 5 minutes about what they have learned from the rounds about the text(s) as a whole. This might be followed by a Go-Round asking each member to share one observation or insight. In a group with some history and trust, the facilitator might ask volunteers to share something they heard from someone else that they found surprising, moving, or provocative.

Facilitation Tips

When the facilitator keeps the time, he or she risks feeling like an intrusive announcer—"May I have your attention, please—time to switch presenters!"—or the caller in a square dance—"Readyyy? SWITCH presenters!" However, when the groups do their own timing, there is the probability that they will finish at different times. There is also the risk that they will succumb to the temptation to dispense with artificiality. But without the artifice, Final Word becomes a small-group discussion, which is a different learning vehicle.

Groups may be bigger than three, and bigger groups raise more viewpoints and more possibility of hearing diverse interpretations. But, of course, the process takes longer, with more rounds as well as more time per round.

Facilitators should take particular care with Step 4. This is where presenters can experience really being heard—a crucial (and often unusual) experience for many. It helps in describing Step 4 to say, "It's not what *you* think about the presenter's passage. It's what you think you heard *the presenter* say (and think and feel) about the passage." There are some variations of Final Word, however, that change the emphasis of Step 4. (See the next section, "Variations.")

Some facilitators find it disconcerting that they cannot hear what all the conversations touch upon. We suggest they get over that.

Variations

Sometimes Final Word facilitators ask speakers in Step 4 to provide their *own* reactions to the text passage, rather than reflect on the presenter's. This has the advantage of getting more interpretations into the open, but the disadvantage of not attending fully to any one. However, there may be times when this makes sense. A protocol called Save the Last Word for Me takes this variation further, and offers still other benefits. In Save the Last Word, each presenter only reads the passage or passages selected, withholding any comment until the listeners have first had their turns to comment. Then the presenter's "last word" incorporates not only his or her original interest in the passage but also what he or she has learned about it from the other members of the circle. This variation is useful in encouraging presenters to pick particularly complex or ambiguous passages—perhaps ones that they think are important, but do not feel they fully understand.

LEARNING FROM SPEAKERS PROTOCOL

One typical and very important source of outside perspective is the invited speaker. Yet we seldom take full advantage of the source. The problem is often merely one of format. We invite speakers to speak for, say, 45 minutes, but they speak for an hour instead, shortening or eliminating the time we planned for questions and answers. Or there are questions and answers, but the questions seem like mini-speeches by the ones who pose them, or the answers take up so much time that most questions never get asked. And there are many other common problems with this format.

But it doesn't have to be this way.

Purpose

The purpose of the Learning from Speakers Protocol is to structure the experience of the invited speaker format, so that learning is maximized for the speaker as well as the learners. The principles of the protocol are the same as for many others: to keep a focus, to foster listening, and to provide an opportunity to construct knowledge, both individually and collectively.

Details

The speaker must understand this new format well in advance. The time frame and other details can be negotiated, but it must be clear to the speaker that there is a different format to be followed, one that must be respected. The number of participants can range from 15 up to 100. See "Variations" for how to work with still larger numbers.

Steps

1. *Introduction.* Just as the speaker must know the format and its rules, so must the listeners. In this step, therefore, the facilitator spells these out as part of introducing the speaker. (5 minutes)

2. *Speech.* The speaker delivers the speech as audience members jot down questions or thoughts that occur for them along the way. The facilitator may suggest that they imagine the possibility for dialogue at each of these points, even though the dialogue itself must be delayed. The speaker may pause on occasion for 30 seconds and invite the audience to jot down some notes and questions. (30–50 minutes)

3. *Five-minute warning.* The speaker is given a warning by the facilitator, sitting nearby, 5 minutes before the agreed-upon time frame is due to end.

4. *Huddling.* When the speaker has finished, the facilitator invites the audience to gather its questions and "huddle" in groups of three to five. These groups should be formed based on proximity, though with encouragement to include at least three members per group. The facilitator instructs the groups to examine all their questions quickly in order to come up with its top question, the one it really wants to make sure the speaker has a chance to consider and answer. (5 minutes)

5. *Top questions.* The top questions can be called out by representatives of each group. But all of the questions must be called out before the speaker is allowed to answer any one. (5 minutes)

6. *Answering.* The speaker then answers questions, avoiding repetition and aiming for connections among the questions and the answers. (15–20 minutes)

7. *Sharing.* If there is time, audience members are then invited to share with the speaker ways in which their thinking has been pushed, and to ask other questions. If there is only a minute or two, this thinking can be shared in pairs in the audience.

Facilitation Tips

It is not impolite to structure a speaker's time and to ask that he or she follow a slightly unconventional format. In our experience, many speakers appreciate the opportunity to have more successful interactions with their audience.

Variations

For larger groups, questions can be written on index cards and handed up to the speaker and facilitator, who can quickly sort through them.

This protocol can work for other kinds of learning from outside perspectives—for example, from a film or video where the participants answer each other's questions and provide important guidance.

PANEL PROTOCOL

Alan Dichter once found himself planning a retreat for principals to which a panel of experts had already been invited. Alan's problem was what to do with the experts. The usual "everybody talks for 10 minutes (which typically becomes 20), then we'll have the discussant discuss, and finally open the floor to questions (when there's little time left for any)" seemed a horrible way to spend precious retreat time. So Alan designed an alternative.

He asked each expert to write a one-page case study based on a problem that he or she thought a group of principals ought to wrestle with. Small groups of principals worked on the case studies, trying to solve the problems, while the experts observed their work. Following the activity, the experts were finally impaneled—but now their audience was primed to hear what they had to say about the problems they had brought.

Alan had thought he might need to work with each of the experts on the framing of the cases, but there was no need. The experts really got into it.

Purposes

The main use for the Panel Protocol is to make sure that a group of educators gets to interact meaningfully with some outsiders whose expertise it needs, instead of being bored by "talking heads." At the same time, the protocol's additional purpose is to help the experts think about and frame their expertise so that it best meets the needs of the people they are trying to help.

Details

The protocol takes at least two and a half hours. The overall group size can vary substantially, though small work groups of 4 to 10 are desirable. The panel can similarly come in many sizes, although three to four panelists seems ideal. If the room is very large, a wireless microphone is helpful.

The experts are asked to prepare for the panel by developing a written case study focused on a problem of professional practice. They may substitute, if they choose, one developed by someone else. The cases should be more or less complex depending on the time that will be available for wrestling with them. A one-page case for a 2-hour protocol is appropriate. The cases should be written in a way that highlights the ambiguities and uncertainties of professional practice, and should end with questions to prompt readers to identify next steps. The following, for example, are good closing questions:

- In light of the information you have, what action would you take?
- Was there any action that should have been taken earlier but was not?
- What additional information do you need to act?
- How would you proceed to get that information?

Steps

1. *Introduction.* The facilitator explains the steps to follow, and asks the experts to introduce themselves and give a brief description of their area(s) of expertise.

2. *Case reading.* Small groups each receive a prewritten case, with each case going to at least two groups. The facilitator allows ample reading time, and encourages note-taking.

3. *Case interpretation.* For a 2- to 3-hour protocol, groups get 20 minutes to work on interpreting the case and trying to solve the problem it highlights. During this time, they also prepare a 2- or 3-minute presentation. This presentation should include an answer to the question, "What is this a case of?"—an answer that will help participants who did not read the case to understand the rest of the presentation. The presentation should also include either the group's consensus (or confusion) concerning action steps required, or a short list of alternative steps.

4. *Expert consultation.* During work time, groups may call over the experts to answer specific questions. But the facilitator has coached the experts to avoid giving elaborate responses to these questions, and to avoid providing overall "solutions" to the case problems. When they are not engaged in answering "call-overs," the experts wander the room and listen in.

5. *Presentations.* Following the small-group work time, the facilitator announces the first case, calling on all the groups who worked on it to make their presentations in turn. Following all the presentations on the case, the facilitator invites all participants to react or ask questions. Presentations continue in this fashion until all the cases have been presented and discussed. (5–15 minutes *per case*)

6. *Expert reactions.* After a break, the experts react to what they have heard. The facilitator suggests that they focus especially on the strengths and weaknesses of the various action steps proposed for the case they wrote, and that they take the opportunity as well to point out what they think the groups may have overlooked. The facilitator has privately suggested to them that this format offers them an opportunity to reinforce principles they think should guide decision-making in practice. Each expert gets a maximum of 10 to 15 minutes of reaction time.

7. *Questions and comments.* Participants react to the experts' perspectives.

Facilitation Tips

The facilitator must meet with the experts beforehand. It is crucial that they understand their role and how it departs from the ordinary. They may need assurance that they will have plenty of time in Step 6 to share their expertise, and that the participants, having wrestled with the cases they wrote, will be far more receptive to learning from this expertise than they would be if they had walked cold into an ordinary panel presentation. The experts should be encouraged to use Step 4 as an opportunity to learn what the participants already seem to know and what they seem to need to know.

If the group is very large, it may not be possible for all the teams to report out. Instead, the facilitator may ask one team to report, and give a few minutes at the end for other teams working on the same case to offer another viewpoint or "crucial action step" if one comes to mind.

In handling the question and answer portion of Step 5, the facilitator may encourage the panel to take 5 to 10 questions before answering any of them (see "Learning from Speakers" Protocol). Not only does this allow the panelists to synthesize their responses, often focusing on themes and reinforcing broader issues, but it decreases the likelihood that the panel will get stuck on one point.

Variation

This can work well with just a single case—one that all the panelists agree to, or that they have jointly created.

PROVOCATIVE PROMPTS

Nancy Mohr and Alan Dichter often use quotations from expert outsiders to stimulate insider discussions. The power of quotations in this regard comes not just from what they say about a topic at hand, but also from the fact that they say different things—a fact made obvious in what one selects and how one arrays the selections. If even experts disagree, others feel safer in owning up to and expressing their own disagreements.

Nancy and Alan have used short provocative quotations to stimulate discussions of such topics as working for equity in education, the purpose of teachers' studying student work, the role of standards in teaching and learning, and the things that beginning teachers most need to learn.

Rather than present one way of using an array of contrasting quotations below, we alter our typical format to describe several simple protocols for doing so. Each one should be followed up by an open discussion or a Go-Round.

Purpose

The purpose of the protocols is to infuse a conversation about a particular topic with a quick and contrasting set of viewpoints on it—viewpoints that participants in a learning group can use to help elicit, shape, and reexamine their own perspectives and attitudes. They are often used as a way into a complex issue that is then treated in a more comprehensive way.

Details

The usefulness of these protocols depends on the provocation in the quotations themselves and in the contrast among them. The facilitator selects the quotations ahead of time and has them ready to distribute in the format desired. Time can vary to suit circumstances, but a quick pace is usually advantageous here.

Protocols

1. The facilitator distributes a page or two with all quotations and their sources listed. Each member of the group chooses one quotation, and shares in a Go-Round why he or she chose it.

2. The facilitator distributes a page or two with all quotations

and their sources listed, then invites each member of the group to choose one quotation that provokes him or her to think differently about the topic at hand, and to write briefly an account of the difference. Then he asks them all to share what they have written with a partner, with the partners reflecting back in their own words what they think the difference means. This can be done with several changes of partners.

3. The facilitator prepares the quotations on individual strips of paper then hands out the strips randomly to everybody in the group. Each person reads the quotation he or she gets and responds to it on the spot. This requires having one quotation for each person in the group.

4. The facilitator writes or prints the quotations on large chart paper and tapes the paper to the walls of a room or corridor. Participants, using Post-its, place comments and questions, as they choose, on each of the quotations.

Facilitation Tips

Each of the simple protocols described above can run for variable amounts of time, though the facilitator should be aware that extremely engaging discussion often results from Provocative Prompts, and sticking to the stated time frame can require one's full attention.

Variations

At the end of an extended exploration of a topic by a learning group—or along the way—participants can add to the quotation sheet that got them started, and they can even engage in an additional round of Provocative Prompts as a way of bringing closure. In this round, they might try to find one quote each to connect (more or less exactly) to the expressions "I used to believe . . ." and "Now I believe. . . ."

A group that uses the Final Word Protocol (see above) over the course of an extended period of time can collect the text passages highlighted by participants for that protocol, and recycle them for this one.

Mars/Venus Protocol

Inspiration for the name of this protocol comes from John Gray's (1992) book about gender differences in communication. Beth McDonald created this protocol for a class session of a course for which half the students had read Alfie Kohn's *The Schools Our Children Deserve* (2000), and the other half, E.D. Hirsch's *The Schools We Need* (1999). The goal of the session was to promote analysis and deeper understanding of one's own text, while gaining some understanding of the other's text.

Purpose

The protocol is useful in helping people learn from contrasting points of view, particularly when one of the views is less familiar. It works especially well when a group has agreed to split into two reading groups in order to tackle two contrasting texts—for example, the books by Hirsch and Kohn mentioned above, or for another group and another set of issues, Allan Bloom's *The Closing of the American Mind* (1987) and Lawrence Levine's *The Opening of the American Mind* (1997).

Details

The protocol runs anywhere from 1 hour to 90 minutes, and may involve any number of participants, divided into subgroups of four participants (homogeneously composed with respect to the text read). The facilitator should preselect and reproduce four or five substantial quotations from each of the contrasting texts, packaging these in two different sets with enough sets for all groups.

Steps

1. *Introduction.* The facilitator explains that the purpose of the exercise is to further explore and understand the text each participant has read through exposure to a contrasting point of view. To start, group members are given the set of quotations from the "other" text, that is, the one they have not read. The facilitator

prompts the groups as follows: "Based on your reading of him, how do you think E. D. Hirsch would respond to each of these statements by Alfie Kohn? Would the two agree or disagree? What underlying beliefs of your author does each quotation either tap or challenge?" (5 minutes)

2. *Reading.* The participant allows sufficient time for each group member to read the quotations individually and to think about them privately in the light of their previous reading. (10–15 minutes)

3. *Facilitation and discussion.* Group members take turns facilitating as they discuss each quotation, sharing their responses to the prompt. (25–30 minutes)

4. *Summarizing.* Each subgroup prepares a brief summary to share with the whole group regarding what it has discovered concerning the authors' differences and similarities of perspective. (5–10 minutes)

5. *Open conversation.* The facilitator opens the floor to the groups, asking each group to report the highlights of its summary, and invites others to share reactions or clarifying questions. (15 minutes)

6. *Reflection.* The facilitator asks the large group to reflect on the value and challenges of the activity. (5–10 minutes)

Facilitation Tips

To avoid the potential for a superficial and dismissive treatment of the opposing text, it is important that the facilitator highlight the need to look for the underlying bases for any disagreements, along with potential areas of agreement. When this works well, participants will have a more complex understanding of the issues that are under consideration.

Variation

Groups can be asked to make a chart-paper summary for posting during the summarizing step. Then, instead of oral reporting, the whole group can engage in a "gallery walk" to read other summaries before the open conversation step.

RICH TEXT PROTOCOL

This is a demanding protocol that Joe and Beth McDonald developed to help groups read and understand texts that need close reading, and that yield greater understanding when approached element by element and layer by layer. The text that stimulated the development is an intriguing segment of a longer videotape that Ilene Kantrov and her colleagues developed at the Education Development Center (undated), and that she kindly allowed the McDonalds to use in their own teaching. The particular segment features a group of five upper-elementary-school students working together on a complicated math problem. Among the students is a boy with a red hat. We make reference to this video and to this boy in the steps listed below.

At the heart of the protocol is a theory of reading derived from the work of Robert Scholes (1985). It suggests the usefulness of bumps in the text—points of interest or puzzlement that can cause a reader to interrupt a smooth reading process, and to delve below the surface to explore his or her assumptions more critically. So the protocol begins with *noticing* points of interest or puzzlement, exploring these in an *interpretive* phase, then ending with a *critical* phase in which participants share in writing a particular perspective they choose to apply to the text.

In format, this protocol (like several others) owes much to the Collaborative Assessment Conference described in Chapter 5.

Purpose

This protocol is useful for dealing with a text that is particularly dense or ambiguous in meaning, complex in discourse, or complicated in structure. It enables a group to "unpack" the text (written, video, or still visual)—that is, to take it apart slowly, element by element and layer by layer. One can, of course, do the same thing in an ordinary text-based discussion without benefit of a protocol, but this protocol has the advantage of making the phases of analysis more transparent. For this reason, it may appeal to participants who might otherwise become impatient with the mincing because they do not understand the method behind it.

Details

The protocol is designed for use by groups of 5 to 15 participants. It can run in variable amounts of time, depending on the length or format of the text, but generally takes about an hour. The facilitator provides the text, and must be deeply familiar with it, having read or watched it several times. It is best to use short, demanding texts in any medium. We have used variations of the protocol in exploring a poem about a child's silence in class, a photograph of students taking a standardized test, a brief but rich account of three different students' attempts to understand a complex concept in economics, and the 7-minute portion of video featuring a boy wearing a red hat.

Chart paper or another medium for recording comments and keeping track of the layers of discussion is essential.

Steps

1. *Introduction.* The facilitator briefly describes the content of the text the group is about to "read," and previews the steps involved in the reading.

2. *Reading and noticing.* The facilitator provides sufficient time for participants to experience the text—for example, reading their own copy of a print text, or viewing a video together. Participants are asked to "notice" elements of the text that interest, puzzle, or surprise them, jotting these down as they read or watch or listen.

3. *Sharing.* In a Go-Round, each participant shares one to three elements they noticed—for example, "The boy with the red hat never spoke" or "The poet starts off using some punctuation and drops it completely by the third stanza." Although it is often difficult to separate noticing from interpreting, the facilitator tries to discourage the latter. "A noticing," he or she may say, "is something that we can check the validity of just by checking the text. We don't need any outside information or expertise." The facilitator does not permit participants to comment on one another's offerings at this point. The facilitator records all the "noticings" on chart paper.

4. *Checking.* In this step, the facilitator asks the group if there is anything on the list from Step 3 that needs "checking out"

before moving on. For example, a participant may say, "I didn't notice that the boy with the red hat never spoke. Can we check that out?" When the text is a written one, it is easy to do the checking as each request is made. However, for videotapes, it is best to get the whole list of requests out first, and then check them all out during a second viewing. The facilitator may again have to caution the group to keep the focus on noticing rather than on interpreting. Did the boy in the red hat speak or not? At this point, commentary about why the boy did or did not speak is not permitted. As noticings are checked, the facilitator circles them on the chart paper or puts a check mark by them.

5. *Interpreting.* During this step, the facilitator guides the group in the selection of two or three items from the chart paper that would be fruitful or interesting to interpret further. This is a judgment call based on the size of the group and the time available. The facilitator leads a Go-Round for each point selected. For example, during the round someone may say that the boy in the red hat does not speak because he is intimidated by the rest of the group. Someone else may suggest that he feels incompetent with respect to the problem and cannot find an entry point. No direct challenges to the interpretations are permitted, but the facilitator encourages alternative interpretations of the same phenomenon. The various interpretations of each element are duly noted on chart paper.

6. *Identifying a perspective.* In this step, the facilitator asks participants to select one idea from the text under study and to write about it, based on a particular perspective or theory that they bring to it. The facilitator should define this theory or perspective as "some overarching idea—for example, about teaching and learning—that you might bring to any text you read about teaching and learning, or that seems particularly relevant to this text." For example, one participant may write that the speechlessness of the boy with the red hat provides vivid evidence of how the shy or learning-disabled child may become lost in a classroom where too much emphasis is put on small-group discussion. Another may write that the boy with the red hat exhibits the characteristics of an English language learner, and may well be learning more than he appears to be.

7. *Pair-share*. Participants pair off and share their writing with each other, challenging each other as appropriate.

8. *Final Go-Round*. One at a time, participants say one thing about the whole text, based on their experience with the protocol.

9. *Reflection*. The facilitator invites volunteers to comment on this reading experience.

Facilitation Tips

The facilitator should feel free to model each step by offering an example of the kind of response called for. He or she should also feel free to trim a noticing or an interpretation as needed. For example, someone might say in Step 2: "One of the girls seems to be just doing the scribing. She is the group's secretary, but is not doing any math learning. Typical pattern for many girls in math." And the facilitator might respond, "At the level of just noticing, let's say at this point that the shorter girl does much of the group's writing but little of its math talking. Somebody can ask us to check that out in the next step if they want. And in still another step, somebody can offer an interpretation of what's going on here and why."

Variation

After completing Step 1, a large group (for example, 12 to 15) might break into work groups of three or four each to complete subsequent steps, recording their results as they go. They might also attempt to create a joint perspective in Step 6. Then small groups could combine to share (and challenge) each other's perspectives, or each small group could real aloud its final result to the whole group, inviting questions and comments.

CHAPTER 4

Working on Problems of Practice

Professional educators solve problems of practice continually, often hundreds in a single day. We sometimes solve them in ways that seem definitive, as when we finally decide which text we'll adopt for a particular course, for example, or finally move Jason out of Ms. Harwich's class, or discover a new way to help Olivia learn to write better. Still, we are not surprised when our "definitive" solutions come undone, or when they generate one or more other problems. In a famous essay in the *Harvard Educational Review,* Magdalene Lampert (1985) proposes that most of the problems we confront in practice are really dilemmas. They present options that seem irreconcilable: whether to punish or forgive, whether to press all the way or yield, whether to believe or to doubt, whether to insist on the detail or overlook it, and so on. In practice, though, the educator manages to reconcile the irreconcilable, often by alternating emphases—pressing to a point and then yielding, being tough in public and forgiving in private. Even as she manages her problems in this way, however, the teacher or principal or dean is chronically aware that one day's wise move may be another day's foolish one, and that either day's move may come to seem either wise or foolish given a certain shift of context.

Thus all of us find ourselves solving problems provisionally, and again and again. This inescapable condition of our work can make us feel like Sisyphus rolling his rock, particularly when we confront most of our problems in isolation. In such circumstances, we run low on creative approaches even while the problems never run low on novel ways of presenting themselves. Meanwhile, the people on whose behalf we must address the problems come and go endlessly, blithely ignorant of the troubles they cause. Who is the teacher who has not on occasion thought to herself, "Oh, no, another group of eighth graders!" Who is the dean who has not thought, "When will this faculty ever get it?"

In this chapter, we describe some protocols that help educators sustain courage in the face of predictably chronic problems. These protocols encourage the educator to frame some of the myriad problems of practice for collegial review. The point of the review is to gain the benefit of others' perspectives and thereby inform one's own, to draw on others' creative resources and thereby replenish one's own, and to experience in the process the encouraging effects of sharing one's burdens for an hour or so.

DESCRIPTIVE CONSULTANCY

As the steps of this protocol make clear, the Descriptive Consultancy is not just about getting and giving advice. The word *descriptive* in its title is important. Before participants get advice on problems they have brought to the group, they enjoy the opportunity of learning how others frame and understand these problems. The result is that they often gain insights they never otherwise could.

Nancy Mohr, who designed this protocol, regularly uses it to help groups of educators become facilitative leaders. Over a series of meetings, the educators present a number of problems to each other for descriptive consultation. In the process, they not only get better perspectives on their own problems, they also become better consultants to each other.

Purpose

The purpose of Descriptive Consultancy is to help someone think through a problem by framing it himself or herself, then hearing how others frame it. That is why participants are encouraged to be more descriptive than judgmental. An assumption behind the use of the protocol is that framing and reframing a complex problem is an especially valuable step in moving toward creative, focused problem-solving. The protocol also includes an advice-giving step.

Details

The protocol requires approximately an hour for the exploration of each problem, though overall times vary depending on the number of participants. The setting typically involves either one group of 10 to 12 or smaller groups of 3 to 5 participants each, meeting in a space where multiple conversations can be carried on simultaneously. Groups may consult on more than one problem, each participant presenting a problem in turn.

Steps

1. *Problem presentation.* The presenting group member describes the problem, laying out its different dimensions as he or she sees them, and including previous attempts to address it. (10 minutes)

2. *Clarifying questions.* Other members of the group (acting in the role of "consultants") ask questions of the presenting member. These are meant to elicit information that the consultants need in order to consult. (5 minutes)

3. *Reflecting back.* The presenter is silent while each of the consultants describes what he or she heard in the presentation of the problem, beginning with the question, "What did you hear?" The purpose of this step is for the group to develop a shared understanding of the problem and of its complexity. Participants are asked to pass if their reflection has already been offered by someone else. (10 minutes total for all consultants)

4. *Response.* The presenter briefly responds to the consultants' expressed understanding of the problem, and provides further clarification of the problem as appropriate. (5 minutes)

5. *Brainstorming.* The presenter is again silent while the consultants brainstorm possible solutions or next steps: "What if . . . ?" "Have you thought about . . . ?" (10–15 minutes)

6. *Response.* The presenter responds again, this time talking about how he or she might be thinking now as a result of what has been said. Here the presenter does not so much answer the group's questions as present his or her new insights gained through listening. (5 minutes)

7. *Debriefing.* The facilitator asks participants about their roles: "How did it feel to be the presenter? How did it feel to be the consultant?" And "Sometimes people other than the presenter have observed that they learned something from the consultation that will be useful to them in their own context. Does anyone have something to share along those lines?" (5 minutes)

Facilitation Tips

When Descriptive Consultancy is conducted in multiple small groups, the facilitator oversees the process as a whole—having first modeled the process by allowing participants to observe an abbreviated or full version. During the process, the facilitator should monitor the groups' use of the steps, not hesitating to intervene if they are not being followed. In explaining and monitoring, the facilitator should especially emphasize the importance of Step 3—reflecting back a description, rather than making a judgment or proposing a solution. The watchphrase should be, "No rush to advice before it's time." This is a delicate step for the facilitator who must gently nudge the group to remain descriptive and literal.

The facilitator should also emphasize Step 4, which involves the presenter's listening to the way the consultants frame the problem. "The reason we reflect back," the facilitator might tell the group, "and listen carefully to the reflections, is to acknowledge that people inevitably have different takes on a complex problem. The power of Descriptive Consultancy is in learning from these takes."

Variation

Sometimes it is useful for a team to present a problem for consultation. This has the benefit for the team—say, a leadership group at a college—to become clearer about the problem as they think through how to present it.

ISSAQUAH COACHING PROTOCOL

This protocol was developed by Deb Bambino, Daniel Baron, and Nancy Mohr, who first used it at a retreat for coaches of schools affiliated with the Small Schools Collaborative in Washington State. The retreat took place in Issaquah State Park, hence the name. The developers will always remember that the retreat began on September 11, 2001, bringing a rather unique set of challenges.

This is a problem-solving protocol that mimics the successive moves of a coach or consultant:

- Elicit facts: "Tell us what happened. What's the situation?"
- Listen actively and reflect back: "What I hear you say is . . ."
- Interpret: "What I think this means is . . ."
- Check-in: "Am I getting it right? Is what I'm saying making sense?"
- Probe: "Some additional questions I now have for you to think about are . . ."
- Connect/extend: "Ideas this brings to mind for me are. . ."
- Elicit response: "What do you think you will do about this situation?"

Purpose

Because this protocol models a developmentally appropriate order for questioning in coaching and consulting situations, it can be especially useful for educators whose roles involve such situations.

Details

The running time for this protocol is approximately 50 minutes. The ideal group size is 10 to 15. If the group is larger, the facilitator should divide it into small groups of three to four participants each. These groups then respond *as groups* to each of the protocol's prompts, after a brief caucus, and through spokespeople.

Steps

1. *Presentation.* A participant presents a problem that he or she has been working on. It must be real rather than simulated, and still be unresolved. (10 minutes)

2. *Clarifying questions.* These questions are for information only, to help the "consultants" understand the problem more fully. (5 minutes)

3. *Active listening/reflecting back.* In a Go-Round, each consultant briefly restates the problem in consulting terms, prefaced by such remarks as: "I hear you say . . ." "What I'm hearing is. . . ." Consultants refrain from interpretation or speculation. The facilitator tells them that the purpose of this step is not only to understand the presentation better, but to help the presenter learn from others' interpretations of what he or she has said, and to correct misinterpretations.

4. *Check-in.* The facilitator asks the presenter, "Quickly, are we hearing you correctly? If not, what would you change/add?"

5. *Interpretive listening/reflecting back.* Consultants respond in a go-round to the following prompt: "What I think is going on in this problem is. . ."

6. *Check-in again.* The facilitator prompts the presenter, "How does our thinking sound to you? Does it make sense?" (5 minutes)

7. *Probing questions.* These are questions intended to get the presenter to think more deeply about the dilemma or problem presented. The presenter is advised not to answer them, but to use them instead to push his or her own thinking. The facilitator cautions the consultants not to ask leading questions, ones tailored to get the presenter to think as they do. (5 minutes)

8. *Response.* Here the presenter is asked simply whether any of the probing questions made him or her think differently about the dilemma or problem. The facilitator reminds everyone that the point of this step is not to answer the questions, but just to help the consultants gain more access to the presenter's thoughts on the problem. (1 minute)

9. *Suggestions.* Finally, and only if the presenter agrees that suggestions are desired, consultants may offer some, again in a con-

sulting framework: "What if you . . . ?" "Have you thought of . . . ?"

10. *Response.* The presenter responds with thoughts about "next steps"—concrete, long-, and short-term steps that now seem possible.

11. *Debriefing.* This starts with the presenter, then all participants can join in. The facilitator prompts: "What was it like to go through these steps? Which kind of question was most useful/least useful? Could the process follow a different order and have it work? How does this relate to your work in the field?"

Facilitation Tips

The facilitator should make it clear that the purpose of this consultation is to provide the kind of help that is wanted. Some people prefer to have their thinking pushed but do not want advice, while others really want ideas.

To achieve the main purpose of this protocol (beyond helping someone work through a problem), the facilitator should periodically call attention to the fact that the protocol simulates a consulting situation. For example, he or she might remind a "consultant" to use his or her "consulting voice" (as practiced in Step 3).

CONSTRUCTIVIST LEARNING GROUPS PROTOCOL

This protocol comes from a 1994 article in *Educational Leadership* by Robert Garmston and Bruce Wellman. It is especially effective for working with groups that are faced with difficult questions, ones that are unlikely to be satisfactorily answered through ordinary conversation or discussion. The protocol seems to defuse anxiety because it creates a sense that everyone's thinking has contributed to a greater understanding of what is being explored.

Purpose

The purpose of this protocol is to help participants analyze the different facets of a problem, issue, or question that they have all been wrestling with, and in the process to move beyond familiar or predictable responses.

This activity is useful at various junctures in a group's work. It is especially useful if there is a sticky issue at hand, one that needs some group consensus building.

Details

The process takes from 45 to 60 minutes, depending on the number of "subquestions" used. These are questions that seem to be components of the larger question, problem, or issue at hand. If, for example, a group of teachers is wrestling with the question of whether to require all third graders to keep portfolios of their work, then one subquestion might be "What *is* a portfolio anyway?" The facilitator must be prepared with a list of tentative subquestions, but should also be alert to the possibility that new (and more relevant) subquestions are likely to emerge as the protocol moves forward.

The participants work in groups of five. Chart paper and markers are needed for recording.

Steps

1. *Introduction.* In their small groups of five, participants assign themselves a number from 1 to 5. The facilitator then explains that the groups will be asked a series of questions that they must answer. These are questions related to the larger question (or problem, issue) at hand. They will be given 5 minutes to wrestle with each question, then one person will be called on (by number) to report their group's answer. Since they will never know which number is to be called, everyone must be ready to answer at any time.

2. *First subquestion.* The facilitator asks the first subquestion, and gives them a time limit within which they must answer it, for example, 5 minutes.

3. *Responses.* The facilitator gives a 1-minute warning before time is up so that the participants have a chance to prepare their answer. Then the facilitator calls on all the number 1s (or 3s, or 4s) in turn to report his or her group's answer to the subquestion, recording responses on chart paper. The facilitator asks the

respondents not to repeat in their answer anything another group has already reported.

4. *Second subquestion, etc.* The facilitator repeats Step 3 through all the subquestions, creating new subquestions on the spot as seems appropriate.

5. *Revisiting the larger question.* The facilitator asks the group to review what has been recorded and reflect on what has been learned about the larger question (problem or issue) they started with. All participants are invited to respond while the facilitator records.

Facilitation Tips

One of the features that makes this protocol "constructivist" is the facilitator's willingness to construct new subquestions on the spot. When all of the group's responses to a particular subquestion are listed, everyone gains a better sense of where disagreements lie. These then suggest new subquestions.

Variations

This protocol can also be used to explore a complex issue or question before different viewpoints on it have yet emerged. And it can be used to tie up loose ends at the end of a meeting, concerning unanswered questions and concerns.

SUCCESS ANALYSIS PROTOCOL

Educators can gain much by collaboratively analyzing experiences of failure—when the plan fell apart, when the students' reactions were not at all what was expected, and so on. The point of this protocol, however, designed by Daniel Baron, Co-Director of the National School Reform Faculty, is to give equal attention after the fact to experiences of success. Here the "problem of practice" is to understand more fully in such cases why things go right. This is especially important because most cases of success in professional practice are examples of successful problem-solving.

Purpose

The purpose of the Success Analysis Protocol is to engage colleagues in collaborative analysis of cases from practice in order to understand the circumstances and actions that make them successful ones, and then to apply this understanding to future practice.

Details

Twelve to 30 participants work in small groups of 3 to 6. Chart paper should be available. Participants need to be able to take notes. The size of the small groups will determine the length of the activity, with variations of 1 to 2 hours.

Steps

1. *Preparing a case.* Each participant is asked to reflect on and write (in the form of notes for himself or herself) a short case describing one area where he or she is finding success or making progress in practice. The case should include specific details concerning his or her own involvement in it—what he or she did that may have contributed to its success. It should also account for other factors that may underlie the success, including any favorable conditions present. (This step may be done in advance of the meeting.) (10 minutes)

2. *Sharing.* In small groups (3–6), the first person shares orally his or her case of successful practice, while others take notes. (5 minutes)

3. *Analysis and discussion.* The group reflects on the success. Participants offer their own insights into what made this case of practice successful. They discuss specifically what they think the presenter may have done to contribute to success, and they also name what they take to be other factors involved. The presenter is encouraged to participate and is prodded through questioning. (5 minutes)

4. *Repeating the pattern.* Repeat Steps 2 and 3 for each member of the group.

5. *Compilation.* The group then compiles on chart paper a list

of specific successful behaviors and underlying principles that seem characteristic of the cases presented. (5 minutes)

6. *Reporting out.* If there are multiple small groups, the groups report out in some way, for example by means of posting lists around the room and "gallery walking" to read all the lists. (5 minutes)

7. *Discussion.* The facilitator prompts a general discussion with the questions, "Do the lists have elements in common? Do any contain behaviors or underlying principles that surprised you?"(10 minutes)

8. *Debriefing.* Still in the large group, the facilitator asks, "How might we apply what we have learned in this protocol to other parts of our work? How might students use this protocol or a variation of it to reflect on their work?"

Facilitation Tips

If participants are asked to prepare their cases of success in advance, the facilitator should give them a few minutes to review their notes. This will ensure that people are focused and provide those who did not actually prepare a chance to develop their thinking.

It sometimes helps people new to this protocol to have the facilitator join in, presenting a case also—perhaps a case of successful facilitation. This can be done in "fishbowl" fashion, with one small group participating and the others observing.

When participants make generalized statements (e.g., "We had a small group of teachers meeting to review our new homework policy"), the facilitator should remind them to say what they did themselves, since this is helpful in demystifying success.

Variation

The facilitator may ask that everyone focus on the same theme (e.g., a successful staff meeting, a successful peer observation, or a successful project design). Small groups compile a composite list and report out. The facilitator then leads a general discussion about common successful practices.

TUNING PROTOCOL

The Tuning Protocol and adaptations of it are often used when professional educators study student work together (Allen, 1998; Blythe, Allen, & Powell, 1999). In Chapter 5, for example, we present an adaptation of the Tuning Protocol called the New York Peer Review Protocol that serves this function for the New York State Academy of Teaching and Learning. However, the roots of the Tuning Protocol are in the collaborative exploration of educators' problems. It was first used, as you may recall from the Preface, as a way to gain feedback on high school redesign efforts in progress. Then it gained prominence when a major statewide school reform effort in California adopted it as a method of sharing reform work in progress (Kammer, 1998). Its versatility as a learning tool for educators depends on two design features that particularly resonate with educators educating themselves. One is the separation of presentation and response. The other is the separation of "warm" and "cool" response.

In a 1993 *Phi Delta Kappan* article, Joe McDonald described the strange sensation of watching a video of student exhibitions that he had witnessed in person several months before. He used the word "warm" to describe his reaction to the exhibitions in person, when he felt himself caught up in the anticipation and pleasure of the parents, teachers, and students themselves; and he used "cool" (borrowing from Marshall McLuhan, 1964) to signify the difference that time and the medium made. Shortly after making this distinction, Joe and his colleagues faced the prospect of designing the Boston meeting described in the Preface. Might it be possible, they wondered, to simulate the cool perspective without the time lag and the videotape?

Ultimately the terms *warm* and *cool* signify Peter Elbow's (1986) older distinction between believing in ideas, people, projects and doubting them. Good thinking depends, Elbow says, on systematically alternating these mental moves.

Although David Allen was not present at the debut of the Tuning Protocol, he played a crucial role in developing and popularizing it through his teaching and writing. Having worked at the Coalition of Essential Schools, the Annenberg Institute, and Harvard Project Zero, David managed to find room for this protocol within a huge variety of school reform projects.

Purpose

As a problem-solving tool, the Tuning Protocol aims to ensure that educators receive direct and respectful feedback on the problems they present, as well as the opportunity to reflect on the feedback. It also aims to help all participants "tune up" their values through contact with others' diverse and candid views. It forces presenters to frame a particular problem from the hundreds they might select, and to collect and present evidence that bears on the problem. It orients their colleagues to examine both the problem and the evidence from both warm and cool perspectives.

Details

The Tuning Protocol takes 45 minutes to an hour or more, and usually involves 6 to 12 participants. It is sometimes used, however, by groups as large as 30. Presenters might share relevant supporting materials, which may include documents in paper or video format.

Steps

1. *Introduction.* The facilitator briefly introduces the protocol goals and norms and distributes a copy of the steps.

2. *Presentation.* The presenter shares the problem, or a draft of a plan currently under development, and provides relevant information about efforts to date. The presenter may also highlight particular questions that he or she would like the respondents to address, drawing on documents as appropriate to support the presentation. During this step, respondents may not speak. (10–15 minutes)

3. *Response (warm and cool feedback).* Respondents note their warm and cool reactions to what the presenter has said. Warm

reactions emphasize the strength of the presenter's views of the problem and his or her particular approaches to solving it. Cool reactions emphasize problematic aspects of these. Often cool reactions come in the form of questions: "I'm wondering why you chose to . . ." or "I'm curious about your interpretation of the parental reaction. Could you say more?" During this step, the presenter may not speak. He or she is encouraged instead to take notes, and in the process to consider which responses to comment on and which to let pass. In some versions of the Tuning Protocol, participants are invited to offer warm reactions first, then cool. In other versions, participants are encouraged to mix warm and cool (though never in the same response). (10 minutes)

4. *Reaction.* The presenter reacts to any responses he or she chooses to react to. The presenter is reminded that the response is not meant to answer questions but to talk about her or his thinking. During this step, respondents may not speak. (10 minutes)

5. *Conversation.* Presenter and respondents engage in open conversation. (10–15 minutes)

6. *Debriefing.* Participants reflect on the process and explore ways to use the protocol in other situations. The facilitator may ask, "How did it feel hearing warm and cool feedback? How did it feel not being able to respond to the feedback? How can you apply this protocol in your ordinary work?"

Facilitation Tips

Each step of the protocol requires a prespecified allotment of time (though not necessarily those suggested above). The facilitator must therefore watch the clock. In some versions of the protocol, facilitators simply facilitate. In other versions, they are permitted to offer responses, typically to redress an imbalance between warm and cool comments. In such cases, however, facilitators must make sure that they do not dominate. A good rule of thumb in this regard is that the facilitator should never be the first to offer either a warm or a cool comment. Another is that he or she should refrain from offering more than one of each unless absolutely necessary to redress an imbalance.

The facilitator should advise the presenter to respond to the warm as well as the cool reactions. Indeed, the facilitator should take care throughout the protocol—in his or her introductory remarks and responses—to suggest that warm reactions are not simply a prologue to cool ones, that both warm and cool reactions deserve thoughtful attention from presenter and respondents.

The facilitator should be prepared to interrupt tactfully when a participant violates the protocol—for example, by speaking out of turn, or by mixing warm and cool, or by jumping to cool when the variation calls for warm to be handled first.

Variation

In some versions of the protocol there is an added step following the presentation. Here respondents ask "clarifying questions." The facilitator must ensure that these do not cross the boundary into warm or cool reactions. He or she may say, for example, that a particular clarifying question might be better saved for the next round.

With small groups and abbreviated timing, each participant can have his or her presentation—that is, problem statement and concerns—"tuned" in less than an hour. In this fashion, the Tuning Protocol can be used in classrooms as a device whereby students offer each other feedback on their work.

We have also sometimes used the Tuning Protocol as a feedback mechanism following lengthy professional retreats, where the presentation is the retreat itself, and the problem is how to improve the format for the next time. Hearing the reaction by retreat organizers provides a wonderful opportunity for transparency and serves to help participants increase their sophistication regarding retreat design.

PEELING THE ONION

In her work consulting with groups of educators, Nancy Mohr discovered that the questions participants brought to such activities as the Descriptive Consultancy were often "surface" ones. By the end of the consultation, everyone would discover that the starting question was not the "real" one. So years ago Nancy developed this protocol to deal explicitly with this phenomenon.

Purpose

The purpose of Peeling the Onion is to provide a structured way to develop an appreciation for the complexity of a problem. This is done in order to avoid the inclination of many groups to start out immediately "solving" the problem at hand (which may not be the real problem at all).

Details

This takes approximately 40 minutes and is best done in a group of 10 to 12 members.

Steps

1. *Sharing the problem.* Someone agrees to share a problem that they would like help with. (7 minutes)

2. *Clarifying questions.* Only clarifying questions may be asked—ones that elicit brief additional explanation. (3 minutes)

3. *Active listening.* The facilitator leads a Go-Round in which everyone completes the statement: "I understand the problem to be. . . ." The presenter stays silent and takes notes. (6 minutes)

4. *Peeling/probing.* The facilitator leads another Go-Round in which everyone gets to pose additional questions raised by having heard the first round. (6 minutes)

5. *Response.* The facilitator invites a response from the presenter as follows: "Having heard these questions, please share any new thoughts about the problem you presented." (5–10 minutes)

6. *Open conversation.* If time permits, the group might now be invited to have an open conversation.

7. *Debriefing.* The facilitator prompts: "How was this like peeling an onion? Why did we do this activity? What other 'onions' are there to peel in our work together?"

Facilitation Tips

The facilitator should start by saying: "Most of us are eager to solve problems before we truly understand their depth. This protocol is designed to help us peel away the layers in order to see that most problems are not simpleminded and require more than our initial 'take' on what should be done."

The facilitator should keep to the times strictly and gently correct people whenever they offer solutions instead of continuing to unpack the problem.

JAPANESE LESSON STUDY

Among the most important problems that professional educators must solve are those concerned with the design of teaching. In contrast to what is often the norm in the United States, teachers in Japan (at least at the elementary school level) collaborate with colleagues in the design of lesson plans, developing and refining them carefully over time. This process is called *jugyu kenkyuu,* or lesson study. In their 1999 book based on an analysis of video data from the Third International Mathematics and Science Study (TIMMS), James Stigler and James Hiebert describe the steps of Lesson Study. The protocol below is adapted from their description.

We first heard about Japanese Lesson Study from Professor Manabu Sato of Tokyo University, who visited the United States frequently in the early 1990s just as the passion to devise new curriculum and learning standards was beginning to wax. In those days, new standards devised by states and subject-based professional associations were often promoted as a means of saving the American economy from the onslaught of Japanese competition. In a series of papers and talks in English, Professor Sato suggested, however, that standards by themselves would likely make little difference. The success of Japanese elementary schools, he claimed, has much more to do with habits of collaborative professional development among Japanese teachers—often on a voluntary basis—than it does with the imposition and control of a national curriculum. Indeed, he argued, collaborative professional development acts in the Japanese context as a crucial counterweight to strong bureaucratic controls (Sato, 1992).

Stigler and Hiebert (1999) offer a highly accessible description of *jugyu kenkyuu* for the benefit of non-Japanese educators. Another good source of information about Lesson Study is a 2002 article by Tad Watanabe in *Educational Leadership.* He is an American mathematics educator who spent 7 months in Japan studying the practice. Finally, there is the chapter by Nobuo K. Shimahara in Gary DeCoker's 2002 book comparing Japanese and U.S. schooling and school reform. Shimahara suggests that Lesson Study is intimately associated with two other features of Japanese schooling: the role that teachers play in what he calls the "cooperative management" of schools (p. 113), and also the work of independent and voluntary national teacher networks, which focus on the improvement of practice through sharing and critiquing.

American equivalents of Japanese Lesson Study are still rare for a number of reasons, including the American tradition of teaching "privacy"—planning alone and teaching alone. In Japan, by contrast, teachers are more likely to spend their planning time in common space that becomes what Steven Gump (2002) calls the heart of the school. Another reason why lesson study is still rare here is that teacher networks in the United States have not tended to promote anything quite like it. Exceptions have been the small-scale teacher study groups described by Helen Featherstone (1998) and Eleanor Duckworth (1997), and the large-scale National Writing Project (Lieberman & Wood, 2003). Recently, however, other networks have followed the lead of these, and many of the protocols we describe in this book are the result of their work. There are signs, too, of an emerging recognition by policymakers and policy researchers that the success of reform policy may ultimately depend on the creation of opportunities for teacher study (Cohen & Hill, 2001).

One result of such developments is that a number of American educators and educational institutions have begun to adapt Japanese Lesson Study to their own contexts. We offer the following "classic" version of Lesson Study (based on Stigler and Hiebert's account), but we also encourage lots of different kinds of adaptation.

Purpose

The obvious purpose of this protocol is to design better lessons and to improve existing ones. In the process, however, it serves other purposes, too. It provides teachers at any level with an opportunity to be continuing learners of their subjects, and to add new skills to their teaching repertoire. In the Japanese context, it also serves as a laboratory for the further development and refinement of a whole school's pedagogy (Stigler & Hiebert, 1999).

Details

As described below, Japanese Lesson Study takes 2 or more hours per session, with sessions held regularly over the course of many months, and study group membership consistent. Some of the steps listed below can take many sessions to complete. Groups are led by classroom teachers, though administrators and others are sometimes members. An important premise of the protocol is that the members share a common curriculum framework, and also a sense of the teacher's craft as involving the creative interpretation of curriculum. The "lessons" involved are actually what American teachers would call unit plans (Watanabe, 2002).

Steps

1. *Problem selection.* The Study Group sets the problem to be worked on—one that has arisen in the practice of several teachers, and seems important within a particular curricular context. The problem might be one that a schoolwide committee has designated for special inquiry, or that a cadre of teachers at a grade level finds perplexing.

2. *Lesson design.* Drawing on published accounts of other teachers' practice and group members' stories from practice, the group designs a new lesson that seems likely to address the problem effectively. The design process is not complete until every member has invested in it and regards the result as promising. The goal of the design process "is not only to produce an effective lesson but also to understand why and how the lesson works to promote understanding among students" (Stigler & Hiebert, 1999, p. 113).

3. *Simulation.* One member of the group teaches the lesson while others role-play the part of students. Following the simulation, the teaching design is adjusted as needed.

4. *Test run.* Then another member of the group teaches the lesson to his or her own students while the rest of the group observes. The observations are not considered to be observations of the teacher's work, but of the Study Group's work. The members of the group typically walk around the classroom to view student work at close hand. Note that in Japanese education, teachers may leave their classes in the charge of appointed student monitors while they observe a colleague as part of Lesson Study. Adapting to the American context, one or two members of the study group might observe the lesson and either take careful notes or videotape it for the benefit of the others.

5. *Critique.* On the same day as the lesson is piloted, the Study Group meets to critique the results. The protocol requires that the teacher who piloted the lesson speak first and in an uninterrupted fashion, describing how the lesson worked from his or her unique perspective and what problems of design surfaced. Then other members add any other design problems that they noticed. The conversation is resolutely focused on the design of the lesson rather than on the teacher's performance in teaching it.

6. *Revision.* Based on the critique, the Study Group revises the lesson design. They may base the revisions on evidence of students' misunderstanding as gleaned from the students' responses in class or other work (Stigler & Hiebert, 1999).

7. *Second test run.* The revised lesson is next taught by another teacher to his or her own class. In the Japanese tradition, the whole faculty is often invited to observe this second test run. As

in the first test run, the results are critiqued on the same day, with the teacher speaking first, and others invited to add design problems they may have noticed.

8. *Final revision.* The Study Group then invites other colleagues and sometimes outside experts to participate in the final revision of the lesson plan. Following this revision, the group publishes the lesson in an internal or external report. Sometimes the lessons are also reported at "Lesson Fairs" (Stigler & Hiebert, 1999). For an American version of a lesson fair, see the New York Peer Review Protocol described in Chapter 5.

Facilitation Tips

As noted above, some of the steps are really phases of a design process and cannot be completed in a single session. For this reason, the facilitator of any particular session must be one of the members of the group, though more than one member may rotate into the role. He or she must have a sense of the group's history, not just as Study Group but as Study Group studying the particular problem at hand. He or she must also have a well-developed sense that it is indeed problem-solving that defines the group's mission, not just design. The point of the design is to solve a problem. Such an orientation is crucial to ensure that the designs are evaluated in terms of their effectiveness rather than their elegance.

Meanwhile, the facilitator is important in developing and protecting a group culture that prizes the slow and careful working out of a problem through lesson design—a culture that is contrapuntal (within the American context, at least) to the one of quick problem-solving characteristic of the rest of school life. It is this counterpoint that makes the protocol more than a problem-solving tool, but a professional development tool as well.

CHAPTER 5

Exploring Student Work

A group of Connecticut teachers from the largely rural and poor southeast quadrant of the state formed a study group in the early 1990s. It was focused on sharing and exploring student work by the light of the new Connecticut standards. The teachers planned to educate themselves about what these standards (and assessments to follow) might mean for their teaching. At one point, the new teacher study group adopted a logo and motto, and ordered some sweatshirts with both emblazoned. The logo featured two triangles. The first, with its base on the bottom and two long sides pointing up, represented teaching practice. "Like a mountain," the teachers said, "impossible to move and hard to scale." The other triangle, base on top and sides pointing down, represented the state's standards. "Like a dagger," they added, "apparently aimed straight at the teacher's heart." In the logo, these triangles overlapped at their apexes, forming a third and shaded geometric figure, a diamond-shaped one. The group's motto was "Work the Diamond" (McDonald, 2001a).

If chapters had mottoes, this is the one we would choose for this chapter. These teachers knew intuitively that Connecticut's ambitions for educating all its children well—particularly the poor rural students they taught—could not be realized through policy prescriptions alone. On some neutral ground, such a policy ambition had to meet practice, and take serious account of teachers' deepest thinking about teaching, and bring students into the picture—real ones, not just ones imagined in the state capitol or, indeed, in the teachers' lunchroom. The Connecticut group's story is a rare case of exactly this kind of meeting. The Connecticut State Department of Education provided the funds for meeting, but the teachers took charge of the meetings themselves. And with the help of some hired consultants, they learned to work the diamond, teaching themselves many of the protocols outlined in this chapter, struggling to make better sense than many educators often make of the intersection of policy and practice.

As applied to this chapter, however, the motto "Work the Diamond" refers to more than policy and practice. When educators explore student work together, they often deal with other intersections, too. Some of the protocols in this book, for example, involve exploring what we might call the intersection of the one and the many. These protocols engage us intimately in the work of just one or two students in order to sharpen our awareness of the fact that the groups we teach are comprised of unique people who do unique work. They provoke us to consider the ways in which our group-based teaching might take better account of the distinct and different individuals it aims to benefit. Such protocols slow us down and bring us close to others' learning in ways that prove deeply refreshing.

Most of the protocols in this chapter also help us to explore the intersection of our practice, our values, and their impact on our students. Do we look first for errors in usage or for the student's voice? Why? How are we swayed by a compelling point of view? Does spelling "count"? In general, do we tend to think that substance outweighs presentation, or vice versa? Why? How does our calculation in this regard affect what our students produce?

The level of what educators learn from exploring student work tends to deepen as they gain experience, though it may be hard to persuade those starting out that this will be true. The use of protocols we feature in this chapter is for many educators less intuitively appealing than the uses featured in the other chapters. Once tried and then practiced several times, however, this use becomes the one they think of first, and the one they may regard as the most beneficial.

What Comes Up

Simon Clements, a former member of Her Majesty's Inspectors of Schools (HMI) in England, invented this protocol for the benefit of the Connecticut teachers' study group described above.

He adapted What Comes Up from the traditions of the HMI, where the examination of student work is considered a crucial source of evidence for judgments (Wilson, 1996). In its encouragement of perception and its press for deeper and deeper levels of it, this protocol shows the influence, too, of the Collaborative Assessment Conference, which is the next protocol we describe.

Purpose

The Connecticut teachers asked Simon for a protocol they could use in short after-school faculty meetings, the kind that are often dominated by announcements and that seldom focus on teaching and learning. Thus the purpose of What Comes Up is subversive if also practical.

Details

This is a protocol for a 30- to 45-minute meeting of 6 to 20 people who already know each other well because they work in the same department or program. It works best when seats are arranged in a circle. It depends on the facilitator's having obtained two or three pieces of student work, preferably freshly collected from one or more of the participants' classrooms, with each focused on a different subject and composed in a different medium. It is best to choose pieces that seem intriguing for some reason—because they raise questions, seem ambiguous, or appear unconventional.

Steps

1. *Presentation.* The facilitator presents the first piece of student work. Depending on the kind of work it is, the facilitator may choose to read it aloud (a story or poem), to post it on the wall (a drawing), or to pass out copies (notes on a science problem).

Participants attend quietly to the work—listening, looking, reading. (5 minutes)

2. *Question.* The facilitator then asks the participants to consider the question, "What comes up for you when you examine this piece of work?" Participants take a few moments to consider the question.

3. *Round of response.* Beginning with whoever seems most ready to start, the facilitator calls on people in turn, going around the circle. Each responds to the question. No one may speak out of turn. No one may repeat an observation. Depending on how much interest has been stimulated and how many people there are in the group, the facilitator may choose to go one more round.

4. *Conversation.* The facilitator invites open conversation based on what the group has learned from the round(s).

5. *Repeat.* Time permitting, the facilitator introduces a new piece of work, and the process repeats.

Facilitation Tips

The facilitator seeks to create an unhurried, reflective space carved out of ordinary work life. The protocol presses for depth through the gamelike prohibition on repeating an observation as turns go around the circle. The facilitator should insist on the rules of the game, but lightheartedly, giving each turn-taker time to think up a new comment if one is needed.

Variation

One can cross this protocol with the Tuning Protocol, and have a warm round followed by a cool round in response to the question, "What comes up for you in considering this piece of student work?" Warm comments are empathetic, appreciative. Cool comments are detached, comparative.

COLLABORATIVE ASSESSMENT CONFERENCE

Roughly once a month on a Saturday, Steve Seidel, Director of Project Zero, convenes a group of as many as 30 educators in a large conference room on the campus of Harvard University. Called "Rounds," the meetings attract some longtime devotees. After a quick breakfast of coffee and bagels, the educators take their seats in a large circle surrounded by portraits of past deans of the Harvard Graduate School of Education. Then one of them presents some student work that he or she has brought. Thus commences a Collaborative Assessment Conference—the home office version of ones that happen now in many other places, thanks to Project Zero's wide influence, and to the availability of two rich descriptions of the protocol, one by Seidel (1988) himself, and another by Tina Blythe, David Allen, and Barbara Powell (1999).

Purpose

This protocol has several purposes, according to Steve Seidel. The first is to enhance teachers' perceptions of all their students' work by honing the teachers' perceptual skills. A second is to encourage depth of perception by demonstrating all that can be seen in a single student's work. A third is to encourage a balance in perception—the habit of looking for strength as well as need. The assumption behind this purpose is that a teacher can address need only by building on strength. A fourth purpose is to encourage conversation among teachers about what the work shows and of how they can act individually and collectively on what it shows in order to benefit their students.

Unlike many protocols for looking at student work, the Collaborative Assessment Conference typically focuses attention on one student's work. This is because of its interest in honing perception, and its assumption that care in looking at one can generalize to care in looking at many.

Also unlike many other protocols, this one does not pay overt attention to a set of learning standards. Still, it involves standards—implicitly, but purposefully. That is because the honing of perception is ultimately and effectively the honing of standards, too, and conversation about students' work inevitably involves "tuning" standards, even when the word *standards* never comes up (McDonald, 2001b).

Details

Time varies from 45 to 90 minutes. A group setting is required in which participants (5–30) have access to the work under study and where eye contact can be maintained as much as possible. Although the protocol can work well with a single piece of work, as long as it is rich in detail, presenters are ordinarily asked to provide several pieces of work by the same student—as, for example, in a portfolio. Typically, participants all have copies of the work presented when it involves, for example, writing or drawing. Other media can be posted or displayed so that everyone can view it at once.

Steps

1. *Presenting.* The facilitator begins by asking the presenting teacher what he or she has brought to the group. The teacher then presents a single student's work, offering only minimal context. He or she might say, for example, only that this is the work of a third-grade boy. Participants read silently or otherwise examine the work, marking on their copies any sections that hold particular significance for them.

2. *Describing.* The facilitator asks the group, "What do you see?" Group members respond by describing components or aspects of the work without making judgments of quality.

3. *Raising questions.* The facilitator asks, "What questions does this work raise for you?" Participants respond with questions they have about the student, the work, the assignment, the classroom circumstance, and so forth. During this time, the presenting teacher listens and makes notes, but does not respond.

4. *Speculating.* The facilitator asks, "What do you think this student is working on?" Responders say what they think the student was attempting to learn, accomplish, practice, or improve. The facilitator presses for evidence to support these speculations: "Why do you think this student is working on . . . ?"

5. *Responding.* The facilitator invites the presenting teacher to speak: "After hearing all this, what are your thoughts?" This is the presenter's chance to respond to questions raised, to offer additional context, to share his/her own thoughts about the

student work, and to respond to any other questions participants may have regarding the student, the context, the assignment, and so forth. At this time the presenter might also share
any surprises or unexpected feedback heard during the earlier
steps.

6. *Reflecting and discussing.* The facilitator invites open discussion, asking participants to reflect on the experience of the protocol by the light of their own larger experiences in teaching and
learning. He or she may also ask participants to share what they
found particularly helpful or difficult while participating in the
activity, and also how they might use the protocol in their own
work with colleagues and/or students.

Facilitation Tips

More so than in most other protocols, the facilitator here
plays the interlocutor, initiating each of the steps with a particular question. Moreover, he or she may use questions to ensure
protocol discipline. For example, if a participant responds to
the question "What do you see in this work?" with an evaluative comment, the facilitator might ask, "What elements do you
see that made you think so?" He or she might also simply ask
the participant to withhold evaluative comments.

Like all protocols, this has a number of features that strike
participants as unnatural the first time through. Here it seems
unnatural to know so little context to start. The facilitator may
have to prevent the presenter from providing too much, and
thus distorting the seeing and responding. Similarly, the facilitator may have to encourage the participants to raise questions
about the work rather than just about the context.

A major objective of the facilitator here—especially when
working with an inexperienced group—is to press participants to
go deeply into the work, to raise more questions and make more
speculations collectively than any one member imagined possible. Another objective is to generate questions and speculations
that cause participants to think more deeply about learning and
teaching. In this regard, the facilitator may on occasion have to
guard against superficiality. For example, sometimes an inexperienced group will respond to the question, "What do you think

the student is working on?" by answering simply, "a math problem" or "an art assignment," and the facilitator must point out that the purpose of the question is not to guess the assignment, but to speculate about how the student frames the learning involved. The thrill of Collaborative Assessment Conference derives from how much can be learned from a single student's creative work.

Unlike some protocols described in this chapter—for example, the New York Peer Review Protocol—the Collaborative Assessment Conference has no preset time limits assigned for each step. This means that the facilitator must gauge the overall time well, since overall time is always limited, and must also attend closely at each step to signs that the group may be ready to move on to the next step. This is tricky, because this protocol may also demand more than an ordinary amount of "wait time"—for example, to encourage as many questions and speculations as possible. The facilitator should listen for comments that may be more appropriate to a later step. Hearing one, the facilitator should ask the person to restate the comment at the appropriate time. Hearing several, however, may be a signal that people are ready to move on.

Variations

If the group includes some experienced facilitators, they can facilitate smaller groups, thus enabling several simultaneous conferences to occur. For a large group, a useful variation is to "fishbowl" the conference: a group of 6 to 10 volunteers, with an experienced facilitator and a predesignated presenter, participates in the review while others observe. Step 6 should then be open to the observers as well as the participants.

NEW YORK PEER REVIEW PROTOCOL

In Chapter 4, we described the Tuning Protocol as especially useful in examining problems from practice. However, as the Tuning Protocol spread to many reform networks and policy contexts in the 1990s, it came to be viewed also as a protocol for studying student work. In this respect, it illustrates well something we said in the Preface, namely that nearly all the protocols featured in this book can be adapted to nearly all the purposes described in the book.

The story of how New York State adapted the Tuning Protocol begins in the early days of that state's efforts to introduce standards-based teaching and learning. Commissioner of Education Richard Mills had the idea of introducing what were then the state's new Learning Standards by illustrating them with exemplary lesson plans by New York teachers. He also proposed honoring the teachers whose work was chosen for this purpose by inducting them into a new entity called the New York State Academy for Teaching and Learning. Officials from his office contacted the Annenberg Institute for help with this project, and two of us—Joe McDonald and Nancy Mohr—agreed to help.

As we and our New York State Department of Education colleagues began to plan the Academy, we realized that membership could be more than an honor. The insight developed as we talked about a peer review process to judge submitted lesson plans. Our first image of this process was that of a contest judged by peers who would review the work blindly and send their reviews to Albany. Then somebody said, "What if the teacher were there?" What if the teacher did not send a lesson to Albany to be judged, but brought it to Albany in person, and what if the judges were others who had brought their own lesson plans to Albany? What if the contest became a conversation at a lesson fair?

Today, more than 1,300 New York teachers have participated in Statewide Peer Reviews, and thousands more in regional- and district-level versions. Although the state still uses reviewed lesson plans to illustrate its Learning Standards on a website devoted to the purpose (www.nysatl.nysed.gov), it has long since realized that Peer Review has a larger purpose than supplying illustrations.

Purpose

The Peer Review Protocol is designed to foster standards-based teaching by means of a structured conversation focused on some actual teaching plans, the standards they address, and the student work that resulted. It aims to model such conversations as a principal tool of school reform in New York State (University of the State of New York, 2001).

Details

Teachers prepare for Peer Review by compiling what is called a Learning Experience. This is a detailed description of a unit of instruction at any level—from preschool to adult—and in any subject area. It must include not only a narrative of teaching plans and a list of materials required, but also the specific state Learning Standard and performance indicators that the teaching addresses, a plan for assessing student work based on these standards and indicators, and samples of actual assessed student work. As conducted at the Academy's annual Statewide Peer Review, the protocol features a facilitator trained in the protocol, a teacher-presenter, and up to eight reviewers, one of whom acts as recorder. The process, including a follow-up debriefing among the facilitator, the teacher-presenter, and the recorder, takes about an hour and a half.

Steps (Adapted from McDonald, 2001b)

1. *Introduction.* The facilitator gives an overview of the process, sets the tone for the review, and describes the ground rules. (5 minutes)

2. *Presentation.* The teacher-presenter sets the school and curricular context for the Learning Experience, and its focus and purpose, including targeted Learning Standards and performance indicators as listed in the New York State Learning Standards guides. He or she shares copies of or visuals concerning any tools associated with the Learning Experience—for example, assignment sheets, materials kits, and so on; and also samples of student work that have been assessed using an assessment plan. Reviewers stay silent throughout the presentation. (15 minutes)

3. *Reading time.* Reading through the written materials the presenter has provided, including the student work samples, the reviewers use Post-it notes to flag evidence related to criteria (list-

ed in the next step). They pay special attention to the relationship of the teaching plans and student work to the Learning Standards. (15 minutes)

4. *Review.* As the presenter stays silent, the reviewers respond to the Learning Experience in "warm" and "cool" terms, with special reference to a set of criteria, as follows:

• Relation to the targeted Learning Standards
• Degree of intellectual challenge
• Quality of assessment plan
• Power of engagement
• Adaptability to other teaching contexts
• Effective technology integration (where technology is involved)

Warm comments are empathetic, appreciative. Cool comments are comparative, critical. Reviewers may not combine warm and cool in the same comment. They and the facilitator (who may participate in the review) must maintain an overall balance of warm and cool. (10 minutes)

5. *Response.* Following the reviewers' comments, the presenter responds to any he or she chooses to respond to, while the reviewers remain silent. (10 minutes)

6. *Full-group conversation.* Finally, everyone joins in general conversation. The facilitator tries to ensure that any criteria not previously discussed are discussed here. (10 minutes)

7. *Reflection period.* Reviewers have some time to think about all that has been said and to fill out and sign a reporting form that has places to record warm and cool reactions for each criteria. (5 minutes)

8. *Summary.* The recorder offers a summary of the review by criteria. This affords the reviewers an opportunity to revise the recorder's impressions, and provides the whole group an opportunity to test consensus. Is the Learning Experience ready for the Academy, or does it need revision, and if so, what revision, and how extensive? (5 minutes)

9. *Consultation.* Following the departure of the reviewers from the table, the facilitator, presenter, and recorder meet to debrief. The aim of this part of the process is to ensure that the presenter is well

oriented for the work of revising his or her learning experience, if necessary. It is only after revisions are complete that he or she is inducted into the Academy. (15–30 minutes)

Facilitation Tips

Facilitating a full Peer Review takes skill and experience. Among the most demanding tasks are helping reviewers manage the multiple tasks involved—for example, exploring the links among Learning Standards, teaching plans, assessment plans, and assessed student work. Another is maintaining the right balance between warm and cool—not too much of either, but with each given its due. A third is figuring out whether and how to intervene as a substantive contributor in a way that is most helpful and non-dominating. And a fourth is managing the overall tone of the session, and of the follow-up consultation to ensure that presenters feel that their work is appreciated even as it is also critiqued. The goal is that they emerge from the experience feeling stronger professionally and pedagogically.

Variations

Although the Academy adheres to a strict interpretation of the Peer Review Protocol for purposes of admission to the Academy, it encourages groups of teachers in New York and elsewhere to adapt the protocol to the practical needs of their own contexts, and to change the components as necessary—for example, the number of reviewers, the time frame, and the review criteria. Many such adaptations exist. Some of the New York City Teacher Centers, for example, have developed a Mini-Peer Review that takes under an hour. In most local adaptations, the point is to help teachers improve a Learning Experience, rather than judge it by the Academy's demanding standards.

MINNESOTA SLICE

The Slice Protocol for studying student work was first used by the Bush Educational Leaders Program at the University of

Minnesota in the early 1990s. Joe McDonald devised the protocol with help from Jean King and John Mauriel. Since then, it has
migrated to many other contexts. In Minnesota, it was always
part of a larger inquiry focused on a question raised by a school
or district. For example, one year, a particular Minnesota school
district wanted to know what teachers, students, parents, and
other community members thought should be the purpose of
education in their small town. So the Bush Fellows organized
focus groups, conducted a telephone survey, shadowed some students through an entire day of school, held a town meeting, and
collected a slice.

The word *slice* reflects the fact that the student work to be
studied is a broad but still limited swath of work. In this same
Minnesota district, for example, it consisted of all the work done
by students between 12:00 noon one day and 3:00 p.m. the next
day (including homework) in two kindergarten, second-grade,
fourth-grade, and sixth-grade classes in each of two elementary
schools, plus all of the work done within the same time span by
25 students per school (chosen randomly from each of three stra-
ta reflecting achievement levels) at both the town's middle school
and its high school. The elementary work was collected by the
teachers. The middle school and high school work was collected
by the students. Both teachers and students were encouraged to
take photos of work that could not be collected (for example,
silent reading, group work, artwork, physical exercise). All the
collected work was xeroxed once names and other identifying
characteristics were masked, and particular class sets (at the elementary level) and student sets (at the secondary level) were
then assigned numbers. Photos were arranged separately.

Frequently, a slice (here we use lower-case to refer to the cor-
pus of work collected rather than to the overall protocol) is less
elaborate than it was in this Minnesota example. For example, it
may not be part of a more elaborate inquiry involving other
methods, and it may involve only one school rather than a whole
district. For example, at University Neighborhood High School
(UNHS), a small school on the Lower East Side of New York City,
a recent slice consisted of the work done by 15 students over the
course of a day and a half. The students were volunteers who
received community service credit for their collection efforts.

They represented a range of skill levels, but included a slightly higher proportion of special education students than are found in the school's population overall. One of the things the school was interested in learning from the slice was whether such students were being appropriately challenged.

Regardless of how elaborate it is, however, a slice once prepared becomes a "text" for discussion by a group of protocol participants. The participants may be limited to the school's faculty, as at UNHS, or may include outsiders, too, as in Minnesota. Before proceeding with a reading and discussion of this "text," the participants are advised to remember that any slice provides just a small window on the teaching and learning life of a community. Like all windows, it excludes from view far more than it includes.

Purpose

The purpose of the Slice Protocol is to help answer a question raised by a school, school district, college, or other educational program. It is important that the question be one that a broad but limited (in time) student work sample can *help* answer. The Slice cannot *definitively* answer the kinds of questions it typically addresses. It merely provides a text that can provoke useful conversation regarding the questions, one that may lead in turn to new insights.

Details

The Minnesota Slice takes anywhere from a morning to a whole day, depending on the amount of student work collected. In our Minnesota example, participants began just after school, paused following the reading to have dinner together, then convened for the seminar after dinner. At University Neighborhood High School, by contrast, the whole process ran from 9 a.m. to noon.

In any case, the Slice Protocol requires a significant amount of preparation. The first task is to settle on a guiding question. The next task is to take steps to ensure the ordinariness and representativeness of the work sample, the slice itself. The power of the protocol ultimately depends on participants' trust that the text they are reading is both ordinary and representative. To ensure these qualities, we encourage the following elements:

- A tight time frame for collection—24 to 36 hours. Teachers and students participating in the selection need to know how to proceed, but they do not need a lot of advance word on the scheduling of the sample. This avoids the temptation to "load up" the sample with unusual work.
- Randomization in the selection of classes and/or students, though sometimes a stratified random selection makes the most sense. If, for example, a school's guiding question is whether White students and Black students have equal access to a high-quality curriculum, the school will want to ensure equal representation of both groups in the randomized sample. Or if a college's question is whether students are gaining a lot of writing practice regardless of their major, it will want to represent all majors.
- Standardization of the collection procedures. Everyone will or will not collect students' notes. They will or will not include homework. They will or will not take photos. Sometimes a slice-collecting strategy involves a roving photographer who takes photos throughout the school or district, within the same time frame as the collection.

In designing the collection procedures, however, it is important to bear in mind the differences between the Minnesota Slice protocol and a research project that uses student work as a data source. The purpose of the Minnesota Slice is to provoke a conversation based on an informative text. The purpose of a research project that uses student work as a data source may be to draw valid generalizations. The Minnesota Slice strives only for a reasonable degree of reliability (across collectors) and validity (defined as ordinariness in the collection). The facilitator of the Slice Protocol should always begin by stressing that the readers cannot make valid generalizations from this sample about all of the school's or district's student work; it can only use the sample to raise issues for reflection and conversation.

Teachers are often the chief slice collectors. However, in slices involving older students, we think the students themselves make the better collectors—mostly because they typically have so many teachers who must otherwise be involved. The trick is to get the student collectors to care about the reliability of the process—either by providing some incentive (University Neighborhood High School offered community service credit), or by offering to debrief them on the process, individually or collectively. Depending on institutional policies, the school or college may have to seek students' and/or parents' permission to include their work in a slice.

Another major preparation effort crucial to the success of the protocol is the preparation of the text once the collection is over. This involves removing identifying characteristics—especially students' and teachers' names—and coding (to ensure that third-grade work stays with third-grade work, and doesn't get mixed in with fifth-grade work). It also involves lots of xeroxing, photo finishing, and compiling.

Finally, there are details to manage on protocol day: laying out all the photos on a large table or tackboard, or along a corridor wall; arranging the xeroxed work at tables that are themselves arranged in some way—for example, all the English majors here, all the Math majors there, and so on.

The details, in short, are prodigious. In our experience, however, so is the payoff.

Steps

1. *Preparations.* See "Details" above.
2. *Introductions.* The facilitator begins with any introductions that may be appropriate, then identifies the guiding question: What is the purpose of an education in our town? Or how does everyday work at University Neighborhood High School reflect the New York State Learning Standards? At this point, the facilitator also asks the person in charge of preparations to characterize the slice. How representative is it? What were the parameters for the collection—for example, does it include photos and xeroxed copies of notes and jottings? The assumption is that a slice will always be to some extent compromised in its representativeness (and sometimes in its ordinariness, too), and that this is okay so long as the readers are forewarned.

3. *Norm-setting*. The facilitator suggests some norms for the reading hour (or even 2 hours for large slices), and tries to gain assent. These usually include a ban on discussing particular work samples with each other, and a ban on talking while others are still reading. They may also have to do with such matters as the order in which work is read, and the pace and character of the reading (not close but nonetheless thorough), as well as the kind of notes to take (ones related to the guiding question, to patterns of strength and weakness, and so on).

4. *Reading*. Participants silently read through the entire slice, literally reading the paper-based work and also studying the photos, moving at will among the tables and display areas.

5. *Seminar*. Participants discuss the slice in a seminar that follows these norms:

- The aim of the conversation is to help answer the guiding question, and the facilitator will periodically remind participants that this is the aim. However, it is in the nature of a seminar to follow its own unique conversational paths, and the facilitator will allow this.
- Useful conversational paths develop best if participants try to build on previous comments, and avoid "stepping on" someone else's talk (that is, starting to speak before the previous speaker has finished).
- Observations and speculations based on evidence in the slice are welcome, but generalizations are not ("It's obvious that there is no teaching of writing going on in the sixth grade"). The facilitator will therefore discourage generalizations, and will also probe for evidence with respect to observations and speculations ("Can you offer an example of that?").
- Since it is a given that one cannot make generalizations about the school, program, or college based on the slice alone, there is no need for defensiveness in the face of evidence-based speculation. For this reason, the facilitator will discourage any participant from providing additional contextual information or explanation ("If we'd only collected the slice the day before, you would have seen a major piece of writing that sixth graders did that day").

6. *Reflection on the question.* After 45 to 60 minutes of seminar, the facilitator asks all participants to reflect briefly in writing on what they have learned from the slice concerning the guiding question. After 5 minutes of writing, the facilitator asks volunteers to share some of what they have written, and invites others to comment.

7. *Reflection on the process.* To conclude, the facilitator asks participants to reflect on the protocol itself and what modifications they might suggest, if any.

Facilitation Tips

The Minnesota Slice puts considerable demands on the facilitator because of its dependence on seminar-based conversation. It helps if the facilitator is practiced in leading text-based discussions. Seminars typically begin when the facilitator asks the first question. It should be an interpretive question, one that is clearly related to the overall purpose of the seminar (in this case, the guiding question of the protocol), and that implicitly calls upon references to the text. For example, one seminar in Minnesota began when the facilitator asked, "Will someone get us started by noting some value that you think you see recurring in the work?" A seminar facilitator must prepare for the seminar by constructing a half-dozen such questions as these, and by anticipating an equal number of possible conversation paths (based on his or her own reading of the text). However, most of the questions a good seminar leader asks are not preconstructed, and most of the preconstructed ones are never asked. Among the spontaneous questions are those that probe for evidence ("Can you recall an instance of that in the slice?"); call for elaboration ("Will you say more about that?"); and encourage connections ("Can you relate this idea to what Suzanne said she noticed?").

One crucial role that the facilitator plays is to help the group remember the guiding question: "Let's return for a moment to our guiding question. Remember that we're trying to understand the purpose of education in this town. What purposes did you see below the surface of this work sample?" Another crucial role the facilitator plays is to help the group mind the norms. So, for example, the facilitator interrupts a teacher who is about to explain how a particular piece of work in the slice relates to a larger assignment. "No need to give us more details," the facilitator says. "We all know that the slice provides a very limited window."

Variations

If outsiders are present—as they were in Minnesota—the seminar may have the outsiders discuss the slice first—say, for 30 minutes—with the insiders observing. Then the process inverts, giving the insiders the chance to continue the conversation with the outsiders listening, again for 30 minutes. The seminar then finishes with an open conversation to which both groups may contribute.

At University Neighborhood High School, where only insiders were present, and where the guiding question concerned the relationship of the slice to the New York State Learning Standards, the facilitator preceded the reading of the slice with an exercise focused solely on the standards. After reading a two-page summary of the Learning Standards, participants were asked to brainstorm what kinds of work they would expect to see in a high school striving to meet these standards. Later, the facilitator began the seminar by asking what the participants had seen of the standards in the slice. After a number of responses and ensuing conversation, he asked what they had missed of the standards in the slice. Following this first alternation of "warm" and "cool" responses, the conversation fell naturally into an alternating rhythm—with occasional nudges one way or the other by the facilitator.

SHADOW PROTOCOL

Janet Mannheimer Zydney, a doctoral student in education at New York University, needed to observe a high school student for a course she was taking, while University Neighborhood High School (UNHS), fresh from its experience with the Minnesota Slice, wanted to see if slicing could be used to get to know one student more deeply. This is how the Shadow Protocol came to be developed. It aims to see a student's work from the student's own point of view, and involves "shadowing" or accompanying the student through one day at school.

In the version tried at UNHS, the shadower chronicles the intellectual tasks that the student faces during the day, both within the formal curriculum and also outside it (for example, in discussions with friends or in extracurricular activities). Assisted by the student, the shadower also collects artifacts concerning the student's response to them. These may include work samples, photos of work in progress, notes of conversation overheard, or quotations from the student's own account of her encounter with a task. The shadower aims for "thin" description—that is, description that is close to the details, with minimal inference and no interpretation mixed in.

In addition to its relationship to the Minnesota Slice, the Shadow Protocol has conceptual roots in the work of "descriptive review" by Pat Carini and the Prospect Center (Featherstone, 1998; Himley & Carini, 2000).

Purpose

The purpose of the Shadow Protocol is to situate a student's work within the context of his or her own complex work life, and thus to understand the student better and teach him or her more effectively.

Details

The Shadow Protocol has four requirements. The first is that the persons who will receive the shadower's report have invited it. They may be the student's teaching team, whose members hope that the report will give them insight into the student's learning. Or they may be a study group that includes only one of the student's teachers, but one who is struggling to understand this particular student, and who hopes that her colleagues can use the report to help. Or they may be the student's Individualized Educational Planning Team, who hope to use the report to understand the student's special needs and to make a plan for addressing them.

The second requirement is that the student (and generally the student's parent) consents to the shadowing, understands its purpose, and actively cooperates with the shadower.

The third requirement is that the shadower—whether an insider (somebody whom the student already knows well, for example, one of her teachers), or an outsider (for example, a graduate student like Janet)—is both a skillful observer and recorder, and also capable of withholding his or her own interpretations of the findings. This protocol depends for its power on the fact that those who commission the data become the principal interpreters of it.

Finally, the fourth requirement is that the shadower and the facilitator stay in close communication. Each plays a crucial role in the protocol itself.

Steps

1. *Shadowing.* The shadower spends an entire school day with the student, noting the most salient intellectual tasks that the student faces (within and outside the formal curriculum). For each task, the shadower describes the student's response, striving for thin description.

2. *Preparation for presentation.* The shadower makes a selection of four to six tasks that seem to him or her to represent a variety of responses on the part of the student. The variety may involve levels of interest and engagement, of confidence, of enjoyment, of struggle, or of evident skill and insight. The shadower prepares a brief description of each of the selected tasks and chooses an artifact relating to the student's performances in response to the tasks. The artifact might be an assignment completed, quotations from the student's account to the shadower of a hallway conversation with a friend, a photograph of the student's involvement in reading or dancing, or any number of other possible things.

3. *Introduction.* At a conference of the student's teachers or other appropriate participants (for example, the student's advisor, counselor, parent), the facilitator explains the rationale for the protocol and its steps. He or she emphasizes its purpose: to understand one student better in the context of his or her life

in school (college, and so forth). Then the facilitator introduces the shadower. (5 minutes)

4. *Presentation.* The shadower presents his or her selected and thin account of the student's day, as represented in four to six tasks that the student confronted and the performances that resulted. (20 minutes)

5. *Questions.* The participants ask any questions they may have, and the shadower responds, avoiding in the process anything but minimal inference and interpretation. (10 minutes)

6. *Private speculation.* Based on his or her reaction to the presentation, each participant (including the shadower) takes 5 minutes to write down several speculations concerning the student's intellectual strengths.

7. *Sharing.* Participants (including the shadower) read in turn what they have written, without commentary or questions from others. (10–15 minutes)

8. *Open conversation.* Participants discuss the entire set of speculations they have just heard. Prompted by the facilitator, they seek to highlight common threads as well as "out of the box" insights.

9. *Planning.* Participants brainstorm teaching strategies that build on their new perceptions of the student's strengths.

Facilitation Tips

It is crucial that the facilitator explain clearly the purpose of this protocol, and remind conference participants about this purpose as they offer their speculations. He or she should emphasize that the purpose is to recognize the intellectual strengths of the student so that these can inform teaching. It is not to evaluate the student's curriculum or teachers. Nor is it to evaluate the student's work or work habits. It may be necessary for the facilitator to "ban blame."

Variations

A variation of this protocol might focus on some other observable pattern besides the most salient intellectual tasks and the student's responses to them. For example, the group that commissioned the shadow might like to focus only on the student's opportunities for learning based on social interaction.

ESP Protocol

In this case, ESP stands for Empire State Partnerships. Begun in 1996, the Empire State Partnerships is a joint initiative of the New York State Council on the Arts and the New York State Department of Education. It aims to increase student achievement in the arts as well as in other areas, through arts integration. Its strategy is the creation of model arts education partnerships between schools and arts or cultural organizations. It is one of a number of successful national and regional networks of teachers that focus on professional development activities in particular content areas (McDonald & Klein, 2002).

To support the 60-odd partnerships ESP has founded throughout New York State, the organization maintains a support network and also holds an annual statewide 5-day summer retreat. The ESP Protocol outlined here is an adaptation of one originally developed for use during the summer 2000 retreat. Readers may notice the influence of the Collaborative Assessment Conference, and also of a version of the Tuning Protocol called the California Protocol (Kammer, 1998).

Purpose

The ESP Protocol aims to stimulate teachers' perceptions of qualities of thinking and feeling in their students' work, to connect these perceived qualities with standards (in ESP's case, the New York State Learning Standards), and thus to help the teachers help their students achieve the standards. Another of the Protocol's aims is to help teams of educators (including classroom teachers and teaching artists) learn how to work more effectively together by inquiring together about the qualities of their students' learning, and by receiving feedback from one or two other teams of educators working on different projects.

Details

The process begins with the efforts of each participating team to select a sample of student work that somehow raises an issue or set of questions of deep concern to the team's work. ESP encourages teams to prepare exhibits that are respectful of the student artists and the media in which they work. Thus artwork must be hung properly and against an appropriately neutral background; music must be recorded well and played back on acoustically good equipment; video must be shot well and with good sound qualities; and so on. In general, these are good admonitions for all those who study student work, but are crucial when the work involves the arts, where substance and presentation are so entwined.

Steps

1. *Introduction.* The facilitator makes sure that all the members of the group know each other, and that everyone is familiar with each team's project.

2. *Presentation.* One team invites the other(s) to observe its exhibit of student work. The presenting team provides no context—no explanation of the assignment or assignments, no characterization of the students or the work setting. The exhibit may involve video, music, visual artifacts, and so forth. The facilitator asks the observers to infer what students are addressing and accomplishing in the work exhibited. (10 minutes)

3. *Observers' discussion.* The observers discuss among themselves—with presenters present but silent—their perceptions of the student work, responding to the facilitator's prompts to begin with descriptive, nonjudgmental assessments of what the work seems to "address," and then to build toward interpretations of what the work "accomplishes." (15 minutes)

4. *Presenters' discussion.* The presenters discuss among themselves—with observers present but silent—the issues or questions that provoked them to exhibit this particular collection of student work. In the process, they acknowledge the ways in which the observers' discussion has affected them. (10 minutes)

5. *Context and standards.* The presenters silently hand out copies of a short written account of any contextual details they wish to share, plus a list of the standards and performance indicators that guided the teaching related to the exhibit.

6. *Observers' response.* After reading the handout, the observers offer a response. Prompted by the facilitator, they especially

address questions of fit and misfit between the standards and the student work. Presenters are silent. (5–10 minutes)

7. *Open conversation.* Presenters and observers are free to raise or answer any questions they like.

8. *Reflection.* Presenters, speaking in turn, convey what they learned from the process of presenting their students' work in this way and explain how, if at all, it may benefit their team.

Variation

Instead of beginning with Step 1, a group might decide to let the presenting team offer some minimal context. ESP suggests, however, that beginning with context tends to tip the conversation toward more exploration of lesson design rather than of student work.

EQUITY PROTOCOL

This protocol originated in the Winter Meeting of the National School Reform Faculty in Houston in December 2001. The focus of the meeting was on equity, and participants grappled with the question of what equity really is—a topic? A lens? A principle?

In this protocol, as in most of the others described in this chapter, we look at student work in order to understand our own work.

Details

The teacher-presenter brings an assignment and corresponding student work on which he or she would like feedback using an equity lens. The facilitator and the teacher meet beforehand and agree to a set of equity-focused questions that seem appropriate. Optimal group size is 9 to 12.

Steps

1. *Presentation.* The teacher presents the assignment to the group, offering relevant context and his or her expectations concerning the student work it may generate.

2. *Go-Rounds*. The facilitator leads the group in several Go-Rounds, each focused on a question. Possible questions include the following:

- What do you see that might be engaging to many different students?
- What do you see that might meet more than one learning modality?
- What do you see that might support/hinder students with special needs?
- What do you see that might support/hinder English Language Learners?
- What do you see that might be considered bias in the language used in the assignment?
- What do you wonder about with respect to equity?

3. *Student work*. The presenter silently distributes some student work samples that resulted from this assignment. The samples should vary in terms of quality, and should also reflect the diversity of the students who completed the assignment. Participants are given sufficient time to review the work. (10–15 minutes)

4. *Final Go-Round*. The facilitator asks each participant to reflect on the relationship between the questions raised earlier and the student work reviewed. The facilitator cautions that the purpose of this round is not to make judgments, but to raise further questions. (5–10 minutes)

5. *Reflection*. The presenter reflects on all that he or she has heard, and comments on any new insights or opportunities that have arisen. (5 minutes)

6. *Open conversation*. If time permits, the facilitator engages all participants in an open conversation, prompting: "What do we think we have learned from this experience about equity and efforts to achieve it?"

Facilitation Tip

One crucial challenge here, as in any protocol where teachers dare to share their own and their students' work, is to ensure that the teachers do not emerge from the experience feeling in some sense "blamed"—for an imperfect assignment, an inequitable arrangement, and so forth. Another challenge is to ensure that the teachers feel free to discuss their work and their students frankly, without feeling that they have to make excuses. The facilitator may occasionally need to remind participants to "avoid the blame game—and the excuses game."

CONCLUSION

Jumping In

In Chapter 1, we introduced a persistent theme of this book with the expression "educating ourselves." We put this expression in the form of the first-person plural to signify that we authors are educators, too, and like all our fellow educators, in need of continual education. We meant the phrase also as a call to join with us and many other educators who struggle to educate ourselves within sometimes indifferent institutions because we think our students' learning depends ultimately on our own.

Throughout the book also, we have used third-person pronouns, especially in describing the work of the facilitator. We have wanted our readers to gain a comprehensive view of the role—from the one who conducts a simple Go-Round with some colleagues on a small task force, to the one who leads an institution's comprehensive effort to study itself and its impact on students, drawing partly on a slice. Knowing that we are likely to have a range of readers with a range of purposes in their reading, we know also that most are unlikely to find themselves facilitating *all* the protocols described in the book.

In closing, however, we want to invite all readers to facilitate at least some of them. So we come full circle with our pronouns. We encourage *you* to jump in. Remember our claim: that we can have the kinds of genuinely accountable institutions of learning that our students need only if many of us who work in educational institutions are willing to learn how to take the lead in educating ourselves. And if *you* have taken the trouble to read this book, then certainly *you* are likely to be or to become a facilitative leader.

How to become such a leader, if you are not already one? The only way to learn this work is by doing it. Being transparent and open about what you are trying allows for jumping in, with opportunities to talk about the results afterward. And the courage you show enables participants to become engaged, and helps build community.

WAYS TO GET STARTED

- Try these protocols in *any* environment. Why not a committee meeting, a leadership team, or a task force? Volunteer to facilitate.
- Get a partner to work with. Partnering is good for morale and for honing each other's skills.
- Seek opportunities to work on facilitation skills through workshops and classes.
- Form a group to support one another, what we call a critical friends group. Meet regularly, and don't just make promises, keep them.
- Try these activities with students.
- Solicit someone to act as a coach—someone who will sit in while you work and give you feedback.
- Observe other facilitators.

THINGS THAT MAKE IT EASIER

- Not skipping norms. Norms can make it clear that you are trying something new and that it's okay if it isn't totally successful the first time around. Make sure one of the norms promotes risk-taking.
- Not skipping reflecting/debriefing afterward. If you don't do it, how will people appreciate or even be aware of what they've learned?

- Not being afraid of silence. Learn to listen. Worry less about what to say. Let the participants do the "saying."
- Being honest about the fact that you have some concerns yourself, but acknowledging that your hopes in the possibilities overcome them.
- Remembering that this is like any sport, art form, or game: you learn by doing. If you try to understand all of the rules first, you'll never get started.
- Really believing that most of the wisdom to be gained will come from the participants.
- Not involving people simply for "buy-in," but because their voices are crucial to everybody's learning.
- Remembering that there are very few mistakes you can make that would be (as our computers sometimes warn) "fatal errors." Maybe mild embarrassment. Think of this as an opportunity to model vulnerability.
- Having the courage, above all, to do business differently, to be a learner, to be a leader, to educate yourself.

APPENDIX A

Suggested Uses for Protocols

	Starting a Group	Opening a Meeting	Closing a Meeting	Working on a Problem	Exploring Issues of Equity	Interventions for Conflict	Understanding Students	Teaching, Learning, and Curriculum	Large Groups	Using Text	Classroom Application
Postcards	X	X	X						X		X
Reflection on a Word	X	X	X	X	X						X
Pair Share	X	X	X	X	X				X		X
Clearing		X		X	X	X					X
All Purpose Go-Round	X	X	X	X	X	X	X				X
Fears and Hopes	X			X	X	X					X
Norm Setting	X			X	X	X					X
Diversity Rounds		X			X				X		X
Marvin's Model	X	X	X	X	X			X	X	X	X
Final Word	X				X			X	X	X	X

	Starting a Group	Opening a Meeting	Closing a Meeting	Working on a Problem	Exploring Issues of Equity	Interventions for Conflict	Understanding Students	Teaching, Learning, and Curriculum	Large Groups	Using Text	Classroom Application
Learning from Speakers					X			X	X		X
Panel Protocol					X			X	X		X
Provocative Prompts	X	X	X	X	X	X	X	X	X	X	X
Mars/Venus				X	X			X		X	
Rich Text					X			X		X	
Descriptive Consultancy	X			X	X	X		X			
Issaquah Coaching				X	X	X		X			
Constructivist Learning Groups				X	X			X	X		X
Success Analysis	X	X						X			X
Tuning	X		X	X		X		X			X
Peeling the Onion				X	X	X		X			
Japanese Lesson Study								X			
What Comes Up	X							X			
Collaborative Assessment Conference							X	X			
New York Peer Review								X	X		
Minnesota Slice					X		X	X	X		
Shadow					X		X	X			
ESP								X			
Equity					X		X	X			

Appendix B

Additional Resources

"Examining Student Work," by Ruth Mitchell, *Journal of Staff Development*, Summer 1999. Presents plan used by the Education Trust for examining student work. Available at
    http://www.nsdc.org/library/studentwork.html

"The Heart of Teaching Protocol Kit," a publication of the Australian National School Network. Includes print material and a 28-minute video showing teachers engaged in looking at student work. Available at
    http://www.nsn.net.au/downloads/protocols.pdf

Looking at Student Work: A Window into the Classroom by Annenberg Institute for School Reform. 1997. 28-minute video. Features students, teachers, and administrators at Norview High School in Norfolk, Virginia, as they discuss their experiences in looking at student work. Available from Teachers College Press:
    http://www.teacherscollegepress.com

Looking at Student Work Resources. A collection of tools and protocols compiled by the Coalition of Essential Schools. Available at:
    http://ces.edgateway.net/cs/resources/query/q/879?x-r=run-new

Looking at Student Work website, maintained by the Annenberg Institute for School Reform. Offers extensive resources

for studying student work. Available at:
  http://www.lasw.org

"Looking Collaboratively at Student Work: An Essential Toolkit," by Kathleen Cushman, *Horace 13* (2), November 1996. *Horace* is a publication of the Coalition of Essential Schools. Describes several strategies for examining student work. Available at:
  http://www.essentialschools.org/cs/resources/view/ces_res/57

National School Reform Faculty. A collection of material supporting the development of Critical Friends Groups. Available at:
  http://www.harmonyschool.org/nsrf/resources.html

References

Abelmann, C., & Elmore, R., with Even, J., Kenyon, S., & Marshall, J. (1999). *When accountability knocks, will anyone answer?* CPRE Research Report Series, RR-042. Philadelphia: Consortium for Policy Research in Education, University of Pennsylvania.

Allen, D. (Ed.). (1998). *Assessing student learning: From grading to understanding.* New York: Teachers College Press.

Applebaum, E., Bailey, T., Berg, P., & Kalleberg, A. L. (2000). *Manufacturing advantage: Why high-performance work systems pay off.* Ithaca, NY: ILR Press.

Avidon, E. (2000). Context. In M. Himley & P. Carini, *From another angle: Children's strengths and school standards* (pp. 24–26). New York: Teachers College Press.

Belden Russonello & Stewart Research and Communications (November 2000). *Making the grade: Teachers' attitudes toward academic standards and state testing: Findings of a national survey of public school teachers for Education Week.* Washington, DC: *Education Week.*

Bloom, A. (1987). *The closing of the American mind.* New York: Simon and Schuster.

Blythe, T., Allen, D., & Powell, B.S. (1999). *Looking together at students' work: A companion guide to assessing student learning.* New York: Teachers College Press.

Bransford, J. D., Brown, A. L., & Cocking, R. R. (1999). *How people learn: Brain, mind, experience, and school.* Washington, DC: National Academy Press.

Callahan, R. E. (1962). *Education and the cult of efficiency.* Chicago: University of Chicago Press.

Cohen, D. K., & Hill, H. (2001). *Learning policy.* New Haven, CT: Yale University Press.

Darling-Hammond, L. (1998). Policy and change: Getting beyond the bureaucracy. In A. Hargreaves et al. (Eds.), *International handbook of educational change* (pp. 642–667). Boston: Kluwer.

Duckworth, E. (Ed.). (1997). *Teacher to teacher: Learning from each other.* New York: Teachers College Press.

Education Development Center. (undated). *Faces of equity, tape one.* Newton, MA: Author.

Elbow, P. (1986). *Embracing contraries: Explorations in learning and teaching.* New York: Oxford University Press.

Featherstone, H. (1998). Studying children: The Philadelphia teachers' learning cooperative. In D. Allen (Ed.), *Assessing student learning: From grading to understanding* (pp. 66–86). New York: Teachers College Press.

Fishman, C. (April, 1996). Whole foods is all teams. *Fast Company*, 2, 103.

Garmston, R., & Wellman, B. (1994). Insights from constructivist learning theory. *Educational Leadership*, April, pp. 84–85.

Gewertz, C. (2002). New York City mayor gains control over schools. *Education Week*, June 19.

Glickman, C. D. (1998). *Renewing America's schools: A guide to school-based action.* San Francisco: Jossey-Bass.

Gray, J. (1992). *Men are from Mars, women are from Venus: A practical guide for improving your communication and getting what you want in your relationships.* New York: HarperCollins.

Greene, M. (1988). *The dialectic of freedom.* New York: Teachers College Press.

Gump, S. (2002). Getting to the heart of public junior high schools in Japan. *Phi Delta Kappan*, January, 788–791.

Himley, M., with Carini, P. F. (2000). *From another angle: Children's strengths and school standards.* New York: Teachers College Press.

Hirsch, E. D. (1999). *The schools we need: Why we can't have them.* New York: Random House.

Ichniowski, C., Levine, D. I., Olson, C., & Strauss, G. (Eds.). (2000). *The American workplace: Skills, compensation, and employee involvement.* New York: Cambridge University Press.

Kammer, J. (1998). Three takes on accountability: The California protocol. In D. Allen (Ed.), *Assessing student learning: From grading to understanding* (pp. 105–122). New York: Teachers College Press.

Kirst, M. (2002). *Mayoral influence, new regimes, and public school governance.* CPRE Research Report Series, RR-049. Philadelphia: Consortium for Policy Research in Education, University of Pennsylvania.

Kohn, A. (2000). *The schools our children deserve: Moving beyond traditional classrooms and tougher standards.* Boston: Mariner Books/Houghton Mifflin.

Lampert, M. (1985). How do teachers manage to teach? Perspectives on problems of practice. *Harvard Educational Review, 55*, 178–194.

Lampert, M. (2001). *Teaching problems and the problems of teaching.* New Haven: Yale University Press.

Levine, L. W. (1997). *The opening of the American mind: Canons, culture, and history.* Boston: Beacon Press.

Lieberman, A., & Wood, D. (2003). *Inside the National Writing Project: Connecting network learning and classroom teaching.* New York: Teachers College Press.

Louis, K. S., Kruse, S. D., & Marks, H. M. (1996). Schoolwide professional community. In F. M. Newmann & Associates, *Authentic achievement: Restructuring schools for intellectual quality* (pp. 179–203). San Francisco: Jossey-Bass.

McDonald, J. P. (1992). *Teaching: Making sense of an uncertain craft.* New York: Teachers College Press.

McDonald, J. P. (1993). Three pictures of an exhibition: Warm, cool, and hard. *Phi Delta Kappan, 74*(6), 480–485.

McDonald, J. P. (1996). *Redesigning school: Lessons for the 21st century.* San Francisco: Jossey-Bass.

McDonald, J. P. (2001a). Foreword. University of the State of New York, *New York State Academy for Teaching and Learning: Statewide peer review.* Albany, NY: The State Education Department.

McDonald, J. P. (2001b). Students' work and teachers' learning. In A. Lieberman & L. Miller (Eds.), *Caught in the action: Professional development for teachers* (pp. 209–235). New York: Teachers College Press.

McDonald, J. P. (2002). Teachers studying student work: Why and how? *Phi Delta Kappan, 84,* 120–127.

McDonald, J. P., Barton, E., Smith, S., Turner, D., & Finney, M. (1993). *Graduation by exhibition.* Alexandria, VA: Association for Supervision & Curriculum Development.

McDonald, J. P., Buchanan, J., & Sterling, R. (in press). Scaling up by scaling down: The case of the National Writing Project. In S. Bodilly (Ed.), *Taking education programs to scale: Lessons from the field.* Santa Monica, CA: Rand.

McDonald, J. P., & Klein, E. (2002). *Capacity for school reform: The role of teacher networking.* Paper prepared for the Woodrow Wilson Foundation, Princeton, NJ.

McIntosh, P. (1989, July/August). White privilege: Unpacking the invisible knapsack. *Peace and Freedom,* 10–12.

McLaughlin, M. W., & Talbert, J. E. (2001). *Professional communities and the work of high school teaching.* Chicago: University of Chicago Press.

McLuhan, M. (1964). *Understanding media: The extensions of man.* New York: McGraw-Hill.

Newmann, F. M., & Associates. (1996). *Authentic achievement: Restructuring schools for intellectual quality.* San Francisco: Jossey-Bass.

Newmann, F. M., & Wehlage, G. G. (1995). *Successful school restructuring.* Madison, WI: Center on Organization and Restructuring of Schools, University of Wisconsin.

Oakes, J., & Lipton, M. (1999). *Teaching to change the world.* New York: McGraw-Hill.

Resnick, L. B. (1987, December). Learning in school and out. *Educational Researcher, 16*(9), 13–20.

Sato, M. (1992). Japan. In H. Leavitt (Ed.), *Issues and problems in teacher education: An international handbook* (pp. 155–168). Westwood, CT: Greenwood Press.

Scholes, R. (1985). *Textual power: Literary theory and the teaching of English.* New Haven: Yale University Press.

Schön, D. A. (1983). *The reflective practitioner: How professionals think in action.* New York: Basic Books.

Schwarz, R. M. (1994). *The skilled facilitator.* San Francisco: Jossey-Bass.

Seidel, S. (1998). Wondering to be done: The Collaborative Assessment

Conference. In D. Allen (Ed.), *Assessing student learning: From grading to understanding* (pp. 21–39). New York: Teachers College Press.

Senge, P. M. (1990). *The fifth discipline: The art and practice of the learning organization.* New York: Doubleday.

Shimahara, N. K. (2002). Teacher professional development in Japan. In G. DeCoker (Ed.), *National standards and school reform in Japan and the United States* (pp. 107–110). New York: Teachers College Press.

Stigler, J. W., & Hiebert, J. (1999). *The teaching gap: Best ideas from the world's teachers for improving education in the classroom.* New York: Simon and Schuster.

Tatum, B. D. (1992). Talking about race, learning about racism: The application of racial identity development theory in the classroom. *Harvard Educational Review, 62,* 1–24.

Tatum, B. D. (1999). *Why are all the black kids sitting together in the cafeteria? And other conversations about race* (Rev. ed.). New York: Basic.

Tyack, D. B. (1974). *The one best system: A history of American urban education.* Cambridge: Harvard University Press.

Watanabe, T. (2002, March). Learning from Japanese lesson study. *Educational Leadership,* 36–39.

Wheatley, M. (2000). Good-bye command and control. In *Jossey-Bass Reader on Educational Leadership.* San Francisco: Jossey-Bass.

Wilson, T. A. (1996). *Reaching for a better standard: English school inspection and the dilemma of accountability for American public schools.* New York: Teachers College Press.

Index

About the Authors

Joseph P. McDonald is Professor of Teaching and Learning at New York University's Steinhardt School of Education, where he oversees doctoral study in the Department of Teaching and Learning. He also teaches undergraduates interested in teaching. His research interests include the policies and practices of school reform, the deep dynamics of teaching, and the creation of new designs for accountability in schooling, including designs based on the study of student work. He was the first Director of Research at the Annenberg Institute for School Reform at Brown University, where he also taught for many years, and was Senior Researcher at the Coalition of Essential Schools. He is the author or co-author of several books, including *Teaching: Making Sense of an Uncertain Craft, Redesigning School,* and *School Reform Behind the Scenes.*

McDonald was a high school teacher for 17 years, and principal of a small public high school in Watertown, Massachusetts. For the last 20 years, he has worked as an "outsider on the inside" of high schools in Providence, Rhode Island, and New York City. Currently he assists in the development of University Neighborhood High School, a new high school founded in 1999 as a partnership of the Manhattan High School District and New York University. He lives in New York City with Beth McDonald.

Nancy Mohr is an educational consultant who directs the New York Center of the National School Reform Faculty, affiliated with the Horowitz Teacher Development Center at New York University. She also works with the Center for Reinventing Education at the University of Washington, and with other projects and groups of educators throughout the United States, and has consulted with groups in Australia. Her professional interests include the development of school coaches, the development of professional learning communities, and the exploration of student work. Her doctoral work was in the area of shared decision-making, and she continues to be interested in issues of leadership governance, especially their relationship to equity.

Mohr was the founding principal of University Heights High School in the Bronx, where she served for 10 years. The school was the first new school to open as a member of the Coalition of Essential Schools. She is the author of "Small Schools Are Not Miniature Large Schools" in William Ayers's book *A Simple Justice*. She lives in New York City with Alan Dichter.

Alan Dichter is the Deputy Superintendent for School Reform and Leadership Development in the Queens High School District of New York City. He is formerly Assistant Superintendent of Executive Leadership at the New York City Board of Education, where he conducted programs for aspiring principals and for future superintendents and deputy superintendents. He also helped to create and oversaw the Executive Facilitators Academy, a program designed to help leaders develop and practice facilitation skills, and he was Assistant Superintendent for Charter and New School Development in New York City. He is a National Facilitator with the National School Reform Faculty (NSRF) and works closely with NSRF New York.

Dichter is a former high school English teacher. In 1982, he became the Director of the Lower Manhattan Outreach Center, a program for overage students who have been out of school. For 10 years he was also the Principal of Satellite Academy High School, an alternative high school in New York City. He is the author of a number of articles on leadership and professional development, and has consulted widely on issues related to urban school reform. He lives in New York City with Nancy Mohr.

Elizabeth C. McDonald is Project Director at the Center for Research on Teaching and Learning, Steinhardt School of Education at New York University, where she also teaches graduate students in the preservice teacher education program. Her consulting and professional development work in New York City and elsewhere have focused on a wide variety of purposes, including the improvement of teaching and curriculum, the support of new teachers, the collaborative exploration of student work, the integration of children with special needs into mainstream classrooms, and the preparation of principals and other administrators for the challenges of school reform.

McDonald has been an elementary and middle school teacher of students with special needs, a professional development specialist for the Rhode Island State Department of Education, and for 9 years an elementary school principal. She is also the author of articles about teaching and learning, and an Endorsed Facilitator of the National School Reform Faculty. She lives in New York City with Joe McDonald.

Download Protocols for Easy Use

The authors of **The Power of Protocols: An Educator's Guide to Better Practice** have developed "abbreviated protocols" to assist facilitators in their planning and implementation. *After you have read the full protocol descriptions in the book,* go online at www.tcpress.com, download the "abbreviated protocols," and customize them to suit your professional development needs. Feel free to edit them—adding your own notes, time frames, steps, and questions—to make them as useful as possible.

FREE Abbreviated Protocols

NOTE FROM THE AUTHORS

The "abbreviated protocols" are designed to be used after you have read the full descriptions in the book. They are not designed to be used as stand-alone guides, nor do they contain all the information necessary to successfully conduct a session.